3,570 Real-world English Phrases for Speaking and Writing Practice

*

Volume 2

-by Everett Ofori

© Everett Ofori, 2019

All rights reserved. No part of this publication may be reproduced, stored in a retrieval system, or transmitted, in any form or by any means, without the prior permission in writing of Everett Ofori, or as expressly permitted by law, or under terms agreed with the appropriate reprographics rights organization.

Enquiries concerning reproduction outside the scope of the above should be sent to:

Everett Ofori
c/o Takarazuka University of Art and Design
Tokyo Campus Building 1F-123MBE
7-11-1 Nishi-Shinjuku
Shinjuku-ku
Tokyo, Japan 160-0023

10-digit ISBN: 1-894221-13-3
13-digit ISBN: 978-1-894221-13-9

Other Books by Everett Ofori

1) Succeeding From the Margins of Canadian Society: A Strategic Resource for New Immigrants, Refugees and International Students. Written by Francis Adu-Febiri and Everett Ofori   © 2009 – ISBN 978-1-926585-27-7

2) Read Assure: Guaranteed Formula for Reading Success with Phonics. Written by Everett Ofori © 2010 – ISBN 978-1-926585-83-3

3) Guaranteed Formula for Writing Success. Written by Everett Ofori © 2011 – ISBN 978-1-926918-22-8

4) The Changing Japanese Woman: From *Yamatonadeshiko* to *YamatonadeGucci*. Written by Everett Ofori © 2013 – ISBN 13: 978-1894221047

5) Prepare for Greatness: How to Make Your Success Inevitable. Written by Everett Ofori © 2013 – ISBN 13: 978-0921143000

6) The Global Student's Companion: 10,001 Timeless Themes & Topics for Dialogue, Discussion & Debate Practice.
Compiled by Everett Ofori   © 2015 – ISBN 13: 978-1-894221-02-3

7) Guaranteed Formula for Effective Business Writing.
Written by Everett Ofori   © 2011 – ISBN 978-1894221108

8) Guaranteed Formula for Public Speaking Success.
Written by Everett Ofori   © 2011 – ISBN 978-1894221078

9) 3,570 Real-world English Phrases for Speaking & Writing Practice (Volume 1)
Written by Everett Ofori   © 2011 – ISBN 978-1894221125

Introduction

Many English learners understand the importance of building their vocabulary, but simply memorizing words is, quite often, not enough. Memorized words are soon forgotten from lack of use. Learners who make it a habit of reading English books, however, are able to retain some of the words they learn as they come across some of the same words, again and again.

Even so, it is shortsighted to focus only on individual words. After all, words come in bundles, or collocations. Already, I have used the expression "come across." If you become familiar with words that usually go together, you can sometimes predict what a speaker is going to say. This gives you tremendous advantage when you are taking an English test.

A collocation, by the way, is defined by the Cambridge Dictionary as "a word or phrase that is often used with another word or phrase, in a way that sounds correct to people who have spoken the language all their lives...." While you should continue to build your vocabulary through extensive reading, you can give yourself additional practice in English speaking and writing by also paying attention to word clusters such as the ones offered in this book.

These phrases have been collected through hundreds of hours of listening to radio shows, television broadcasts, podcasts, university lectures and interviews. Phrases have also been culled from newspaper and magazine articles, as well as contemporary books of both fiction and nonfiction. Here's wishing you all the best in your continued efforts to become a more proficient user of the English language.

How to Use this Book

1	going to go	*(Write down the meaning of the phrase here)*
SS	*(Write down a sample sentence here. SS = Sample Sentence)*	
MS	*(Write down your own sentence here. MS = My Sentence)*	
2	by car	
SS		
MS		

The above pattern is used throughout the book.

If you are certain you know the meaning of a phrase, just go ahead and use that phrase in a sentence in the row labeled MS (My Sentence). If you are not sure about the meaning, search online using any major search engine and write down the meaning in the box to the right of the phrase.

To find a Sample Sentence (SS), you can type in the phrase in a search engine and add the name of a major newspaper, for example: "going to go" and NYTimes

Finally, get an English teacher or tutor to check if your sentences are correct. All the very best on your English learning journey.

1	it's hard to believe that	
SS		
MS		
2	had a discussion with	
SS		
MS		
3	face to face with	
SS		
MS		
4	a shocking video	
SS		
MS		
5	heading down	
SS		
MS		
6	on location	
SS		
MS		

7	a day after	
SS		
MS		
8	a good first step	
SS		
MS		
9	vitally important	
SS		
MS		
10	got hit with	
SS		
MS		
11	in fairness	
SS		
MS		
12	not surprised by	
SS		
MS		

13	a major decision	
SS		
MS		
14	a bunch of people	
SS		
MS		
15	open an investigation	
SS		
MS		
16	follow directions	
SS		
MS		
17	a lot of concern	
SS		
MS		
18	an expert on	
SS		
MS		

19	succeeded at	
SS		
MS		
20	must not have paid attention to	
SS		
MS		
21	first real job	
SS		
MS		
22	miss work	
SS		
MS		
23	a basic understanding of	
SS		
MS		
24	frequent absences	
SS		
MS		

25	recently made an enquiry as to	
SS		
MS		
26	on a roll	
SS		
MS		
27	had no idea	
SS		
MS		
28	could no longer	
SS		
MS		
29	incredibly gracious	
SS		
MS		
30	for numerous reasons	
SS		
MS		

31	ended up starting	
SS		
MS		
32	last-ditch effort	
SS		
MS		
33	stripped of	
SS		
MS		
34	seized the spotlight	
SS		
MS		
35	abased by	
SS		
MS		
36	the leader abdicated	
SS		
MS		

37	an aberration	
SS		
MS		
38	aid and abet	
SS		
MS		
39	kept hearing	
SS		
MS		
40	should not abhor	
SS		
MS		
41	abide by	
SS		
MS		
42	abject poverty	
SS		
MS		

43	abjured bad policies	
SS		
MS		
44	the practice of abnegation	
SS		
MS		
45	had to abort	
SS		
MS		
46	an abridged version of	
SS		
MS		
47	should not abrogate	
SS		
MS		
48	absconded with	
SS		
MS		

49	gave absolution to	
SS		
MS		
50	abstained from	
SS		
MS		
51	an abstruse subject	
SS		
MS		
52	acceded to	
SS		
MS		
53	need to accentuate	
SS		
MS		
54	fount of knowledge	
SS		
MS		

55	the acclaim of	
SS		
MS		
56	need not	
SS		
MS		
57	tough on	
SS		
MS		
58	accommodating to	
SS		
MS		
59	in accord with	
SS		
MS		
60	decided to accost	
SS		
MS		

61	acquiesced to	
SS		
MS		
62	a great deal of acrimony	
SS		
MS		
63	business acumen	
SS		
MS		
64	acute pain	
SS		
MS		
65	an accretion of	
SS		
MS		
66	too acerbic	
SS		
MS		

67	adept at	
SS		
MS		
68	a grab bag of	
SS		
MS		
69	was admonished by	
SS		
MS		
70	adorned X with	
SS		
MS		
71	adroit manner	
SS		
MS		
72	the plan adumbrated by	
SS		
MS		

73	the adverse effect of	
SS		
MS		
74	an advocate of	
SS		
MS		
75	aerial surveillance	
SS		
MS		
76	aesthetic appeal	
SS		
MS		
77	an affable fellow	
SS		
MS		
78	affluent people	
SS		
MS		

79	an affront to	
SS		
MS		
80	a way to aggrandize	
SS		
MS		
81	in aggregate	
SS		
MS		
82	an agile tech company	
SS		
MS		
83	agnostic about	
SS		
MS		
84	with alacrity	
SS		
MS		

85	assumed an alias	
SS		
MS		
86	allay (one's) fears	
SS		
MS		
87	alleged that	
SS		
MS		
88	can alleviate	
SS		
MS		
89	allocated to	
SS		
MS		
90	seemed aloof	
SS		
MS		

91	an altercation with	
SS		
MS		
92	could amalgamate	
SS		
MS		
93	ambivalent about	
SS		
MS		
94	desire to ameliorate	
SS		
MS		
95	amenable to	
SS		
MS		
96	superb amenities	
SS		
MS		

97	quite amorous	
SS		
MS		
98	an amorphous blob	
SS		
MS		
99	anachronistic custom	
SS		
MS		
100	used an analgesic	
SS		
MS		
101	analogous to	
SS		
MS		
102	a state of anarchy	
SS		
MS		

103	anathema to	
SS		
MS		
104	an anecdote about	
SS		
MS		
105	suffered anesthesia	
SS		
MS		
106	great anguish	
SS		
MS		
107	in the annex	
SS		
MS		
108	quite an anomaly	
SS		
MS		

109	an anonymous message	
SS		
MS		
110	mutual antagonism	
SS		
MS		
111	an antecedent	
SS		
MS		
112	the antediluvian era	
SS		
MS		
113	an anthology of	
SS		
MS		
114	antipathy towards	
SS		
MS		

115	an antiquated way of	
SS		
MS		
116	antiseptic instruments	
SS		
MS		
117	the antithesis of	
SS		
MS		
118	anxiety about	
SS		
MS		
119	apathetic about	
SS		
MS		
120	an apocryphal story	
SS		
MS		

121	in order to appease	
SS		
MS		
122	was appraised	
SS		
MS		
123	was apprehended	
SS		
MS		
124	apprehended the main points	
SS		
MS		
125	with approbation	
SS		
MS		
126	was appropriated by	
SS		
MS		

127	an appropriate response	
SS		
MS		
128	aquatic plants	
SS		
MS		
129	arable land	
SS		
MS		
130	an aribiter of	
SS		
MS		
131	an arbitrary decision	
SS		
MS		
132	sought arbitration	
SS		
MS		

133	bought off (by)	
SS		
MS		
134	take action	
SS		
MS		
135	arboreal splendour	
SS		
MS		
136	arcane lore	
SS		
MS		
137	archetypical hero	
SS		
MS		
138	with ardour	
SS		
MS		

139	arid land	
SS		
MS		
140	arrogated the right to	
SS		
MS		
141	indigenous artifacts	
SS		
MS		
142	an ascetic life	
SS		
MS		
143	kind of surprised by	
SS		
MS		
144	aspire to	
SS		
MS		

145	ascribe X to	
SS		
MS		
146	rifts remain	
SS		
MS		
147	assailed by	
SS		
MS		
148	assess the damage	
SS		
MS		
149	assiduous in	
SS		
MS		
150	assuaged the fears of	
SS		
MS		

151	astute observation	
SS		
MS		
152	applied for asylum	
SS		
MS		
153	atone for	
SS		
MS		
154	worlds apart	
SS		
MS		
155	could atrophy	
SS		
MS		
156	might attain	
SS		
MS		

157	personal attributes	
SS		
MS		
158	audacious leap	
SS		
MS		
159	audible gasps	
SS		
MS		
160	auspicious year	
SS		
MS		
161	austere dwelling	
SS		
MS		
162	a life of avarice	
SS		
MS		

163	avenged X	
SS		
MS		
164	aversion to	
SS		
MS		
165	balked at	
SS		
MS		
166	a soothing ballad	
SS		
MS		
167	the bane of	
SS		
MS		
168	the bard of	
SS		
MS		

169	a battery of	
SS		
MS		
170	might beguile	
SS		
MS		
171	a behemoth	
SS		
MS		
172	benevolent service	
SS		
MS		
173	was berated by	
SS		
MS		
174	X beseeched Y for	
SS		
MS		

175	a benign tumour	
SS		
MS		
176	bereft of	
SS		
MS		
177	biased against	
SS		
MS		
178	was bilked by	
SS		
MS		
179	blandish X into	
SS		
MS		
180	without blemish	
SS		
MS		

181	after years of blight	
SS		
MS		
182	boisterous place	
SS		
MS		
183	a boon to	
SS		
MS		
184	bombastic attitude	
SS		
MS		
185	bourgeois habits	
SS		
MS		
186	a brazen attempt	
SS		
MS		

187	asked to burnish	
SS		
MS		
188	brandished X	
SS		
MS		
189	need to buttress	
SS		
MS		
190	a cacophony of	
SS		
MS		
191	the cadence of	
SS		
MS		
192	cajole X into	
SS		
MS		

193	spoke with candor	
SS		
MS		
194	the camaraderie among	
SS		
MS		
195	canvassed the area	
SS		
MS		
196	capacious den	
SS		
MS		
197	capricious behaviour	
SS		
MS		
198	caroused till dawn	
SS		
MS		

199	carped at	
SS		
MS		
200	a catalogue of	
SS		
MS		
201	catalyzed the members	
SS		
MS		
202	held a caucus	
SS		
MS		
203	cavorted with	
SS		
MS		
204	too cerebral	
SS		
MS		

205	chastised by	
SS		
MS		
206	chided X for	
SS		
MS		
207	cherish X	
SS		
MS		
208	astounding choreography	
SS		
MS		
209	a chronicle of	
SS		
MS		
210	chronological order	
SS		
MS		

211	circuitous route	
SS		
MS		
212	speaking in circumlocution	
SS		
MS		
213	circumvented by	
SS		
MS		
214	seemed clairvoyant	
SS		
MS		
215	cleaved into	
SS		
MS		
216	cleave to	
SS		
MS		

217	in such a clamour	
SS		
MS		
218	clamoured for	
SS		
MS		
219	clandestine activities	
SS		
MS		
220	sought clemency	
SS		
MS		
221	the clergy	
SS		
MS		
222	cloying remarks	
SS		
MS		

223	had coagulated	
SS		
MS		
224	coalesced into	
SS		
MS		
225	had been coerced into	
SS		
MS		
226	colloquial expression	
SS		
MS		
227	no collusion	
SS		
MS		
228	a veritable colossus	
SS		
MS		

229	no desire to be	
SS		
MS		
230	commodious sedan	
SS		
MS		
231	compelling evidence	
SS		
MS		
232	compensate X for	
SS		
MS		
233	too much complacency	
SS		
MS		
234	dubious claim	
SS		
MS		

235	got a compliment	
SS		
MS		
236	compounded with	
SS		
MS		
237	a compound of	
SS		
MS		
238	a comfortable compound	
SS		
MS		
239	comprehensive coverage	
SS		
MS		
240	was compressed	
SS		
MS		

241	felt no compunction for	
SS		
MS		
242	conceded that	
SS		
MS		
243	a conciliatory gesture	
SS		
MS		
244	a highly-skilled cobbler	
SS		
MS		
245	X complements Y	
SS		
MS		
246	wholly compliant	
SS		
MS		

247	ought to be concise	
SS		
MS		
248	concocted a story about	
SS		
MS		
249	concomitant appreciation for	
SS		
MS		
250	in concord	
SS		
MS		
251	offered condolences	
SS		
MS		
252	should not condone	
SS		
MS		

253	the perfect conduit	
SS		
MS		
254	variety of confectionery available	
SS		
MS		
255	a confidant of	
SS		
MS		
256	a conflagration	
SS		
MS		
257	a confluence of events	
SS		
MS		
258	a life of conformity	
SS		
MS		

259	a conformist society	
SS		
MS		
260	X confounded Y	
SS		
MS		
261	congealed into	
SS		
MS		
262	congenial manner	
SS		
MS		
263	a welcoming congregation	
SS		
MS		
264	perfect congruity	
SS		
MS		

265	connived to	
SS		
MS		
266	consecrated (oneself) to	
SS		
MS		
267	reached a consensus	
SS		
MS		
268	scare tactics	
SS		
MS		
269	a consolation prize	
SS		
MS		
270	consonant with	
SS		
MS		

271	a constituent of	
SS		
MS		
272	constrain X from	
SS		
MS		
273	consummate performer	
SS		
MS		
274	consumption of	
SS		
MS		
275	contemporaneous with	
SS		
MS		
276	contentious issue	
SS		
MS		

277	contravened the rules	
SS		
MS		
278	contrite manner	
SS		
MS		
279	a frightful-looking contusion	
SS		
MS		
280	quite a conundrum	
SS		
MS		
281	convened at	
SS		
MS		
282	convention hall	
SS		
MS		

283	convivial atmosphere	
SS		
MS		
284	convoluted story	
SS		
MS		
285	copious notes	
SS		
MS		
286	cordial manner	
SS		
MS		
287	the coronation of	
SS		
MS		
288	corpulent cops	
SS		
MS		

289	corroborated by	
SS		
MS		
290	corrosive influence	
SS		
MS		
291	a cosmopolitan city	
SS		
MS		
292	counteracted by	
SS		
MS		
293	coup d'etat	
SS		
MS		
294	take a dim view of	
SS		
MS		

295	began to covet	
SS		
MS		
296	full confession	
SS		
MS		
297	covert operation	
SS		
MS		
298	the credulity of	
SS		
MS		
299	crescendo of attacks	
SS		
MS		
300	culmination of events	
SS		
MS		

301	culpable for	
SS		
MS		
302	cumulative effect	
SS		
MS		
303	a cunning ploy	
SS		
MS		
304	blinded by cupidity	
SS		
MS		
305	a cursory glance	
SS		
MS		
306	curt response	
SS		
MS		

307	curtail participation in	
SS		
MS		
308	a daunting task	
SS		
MS		
309	dearth of	
SS		
MS		
310	the X debacle	
SS		
MS		
311	is debased when	
SS		
MS		
312	debauched reputation	
SS		
MS		

313	tried to debunk	
SS		
MS		
314	a decorous start to	
SS		
MS		
315	X decries Y	
SS		
MS		
316	defaced a monument	
SS		
MS		
317	defamatory comment	
SS		
MS		
318	defer an increase in	
SS		
MS		

319	deferential to	
SS		
MS		
320	defile the environment	
SS		
MS		
321	deft treatment of	
SS		
MS		
322	a defunct satellite	
SS		
MS		
323	delegate tasks to	
SS		
MS		
324	deleterious effects	
SS		
MS		

325	delineate the policy	
SS		
MS		
326	a demagogue can	
SS		
MS		
327	demarcation between A and B	
SS		
MS		
328	not okay to demean	
SS		
MS		
329	a demure gown	
SS		
MS		
330	should not denigrate	
SS		
MS		

331	call to denounce	
SS		
MS		
332	deplore the attack on	
SS		
MS		
333	the depths of depravity	
SS		
MS		
334	self-deprecating humor	
SS		
MS		
335	derelict in	
SS		
MS		
336	unfair to deride	
SS		
MS		

337	require restitution	
SS		
MS		
338	should not be desecrated	
SS		
MS		
339	desiccated terrain	
SS		
MS		
340	desolate area	
SS		
MS		
341	had become despondent	
SS		
MS		
342	an enlightened despot	
SS		
MS		

343	penniless and destitute	
SS		
MS		
344	deter X from	
SS		
MS		
345	a devious burglar	
SS		
MS		
346	speak in dialect	
SS		
MS		
347	a diaphanous shroud	
SS		
MS		
348	a didactic look at	
SS		
MS		

349	a diffident singer	
SS		
MS		
350	diffuse efforts	
SS		
MS		
351	dilatory behaviour	
SS		
MS		
352	a diligent student	
SS		
MS		
353	a diminutive figure	
SS		
MS		
354	a funeral dirge	
SS		
MS		

355	become disaffected	
SS		
MS		
356	disavowed the statements of	
SS		
MS		
357	could discern	
SS		
MS		
358	refused to disclose	
SS		
MS		
359	discomfited by	
SS		
MS		
360	discordant music	
SS		
MS		

361	discrepancy between A and B	
SS		
MS		
362	exercised discretion	
SS		
MS		
363	discursive lecture	
SS		
MS		
364	a look of disdain	
SS		
MS		
365	a disgruntled employee	
SS		
MS		
366	felt disheartened by	
SS		
MS		

367	disparate elements	
SS		
MS		
368	immediately dispatched to	
SS		
MS		
369	dispel doubts	
SS		
MS		
370	gradually dispersed	
SS		
MS		
371	in disrepute	
SS		
MS		
372	dissembled about	
SS		
MS		

373	disseminate information	
SS		
MS		
374	dissented from	
SS		
MS		
375	should dissipate soon	
SS		
MS		
376	dissonance between A and B	
SS		
MS		
377	dissuade X from	
SS		
MS		
378	distended stomach	
SS		
MS		

379	in a dither over	
SS		
MS		
380	divine intervention	
SS		
MS		
381	a divisive issue	
SS		
MS		
382	refused to divulge	
SS		
MS		
383	docile behaviour	
SS		
MS		
384	so dogmatic	
SS		
MS		

385	has lain dormant	
SS		
MS		
386	a dour manner	
SS		
MS		
387	dubious about	
SS		
MS		
388	duplicity was exposed	
SS		
MS		
389	under duress	
SS		
MS		
390	a dynamic relationship	
SS		
MS		

391	an ebullient dancer	
SS		
MS		
392	eclectic taste	
SS		
MS		
393	ecstatic applause	
SS		
MS		
394	a government edict	
SS		
MS		
395	effaced by time	
SS		
MS		
396	an efficacious remedy	
SS		
MS		

397	has the effrontery to	
SS		
MS		
398	the most effulgent smile	
SS		
MS		
399	an egregious example	
SS		
MS		
400	made elaborate preparations	
SS		
MS		
401	elated to be	
SS		
MS		
402	an elegy	
SS		
MS		

403	elicit the support of	
SS		
MS		
404	an eloquent speaker	
SS		
MS		
405	asked to elucidate	
SS		
MS		
406	eluded capture	
SS		
MS		
407	appeared emaciated	
SS		
MS		
408	embellished with	
SS		
MS		

409	embezzled funds	
SS		
MS		
410	emended a text	
SS		
MS		
411	an eminent judge	
SS		
MS		
412	emollient tone	
SS		
MS		
413	to emote	
SS		
MS		
414	bereft of any empathy	
SS		
MS		

415	empirical evidence	
SS		
MS		
416	tried to emulate	
SS		
MS		
417	enamoured of	
SS		
MS		
418	for an encore	
SS		
MS		
419	encumber ed by	
SS		
MS		
420	felt enervated	
SS		
MS		

421	newly enfranchised voters	
SS		
MS		
422	disenfranchisement of	
SS		
MS		
423	has engendered	
SS		
MS		
424	enigmatic smile	
SS		
MS		
425	enamoured with	
SS		
MS		
426	a sense of ennui	
SS		
MS		

427	job/schoolwork entails	
SS		
MS		
428	enthralled by	
SS		
MS		
429	turned out to be ephemeral	
SS		
MS		
430	an epistolary novel	
SS		
MS		
431	epitome of	
SS		
MS		
432	with equanimity	
SS		
MS		

433	issue a notice	
SS		
MS		
434	equivocal evidence	
SS		
MS		
435	an erudite instructor	
SS		
MS		
436	make a point to eschew	
SS		
MS		
437	esoteric knowledge	
SS		
MS		
438	espoused by	
SS		
MS		

439	an ethereal glow	
SS		
MS		
440	etymology is important because	
SS		
MS		
441	a euphoric mood	
SS		
MS		
442	evanescent fame	
SS		
MS		
443	evinced an interest in	
SS		
MS		
444	exacerbated tensions	
SS		
MS		

445	tend to exalt	
SS		
MS		
446	sure to exasperate	
SS		
MS		
447	began to excavate	
SS		
MS		
448	countless discussions	
SS		
MS		
449	exculpated X from	
SS		
MS		
450	a fishing excursion	
SS		
MS		

451	execrable taste	
SS		
MS		
452	out of breath	
SS		
MS		
453	exhorted the children to	
SS		
MS		
454	raise awareness of	
SS		
MS		
455	exigent circumstances	
SS		
MS		
456	was exonerated	
SS		
MS		

457	a wonderful opportunity	
SS		
MS		
458	exorbitant fees	
SS		
MS		
459	backpedaled on	
SS		
MS		
460	expedient to	
SS		
MS		
461	hope to expiate	
SS		
MS		
462	an extremely dangerous place	
SS		
MS		

463	light-hearted ceremony	
SS		
MS		
464	express gratitude for	
SS		
MS		
465	hope to expunge	
SS		
MS		
466	it was essential to expurgate	
SS		
MS		
467	an occasion to	
SS		
MS		
468	a secular holiday	
SS		
MS		

469	held a feast for	
SS		
MS		
470	give thanks for	
SS		
MS		
471	can't afford	
SS		
MS		
472	make better decisions	
SS		
MS		
473	surprised how	
SS		
MS		
474	it is easy to find	
SS		
MS		

475	extant records	
SS		
MS		
476	the equivalent of	
SS		
MS		
477	spread around the world	
SS		
MS		
478	a popular day for	
SS		
MS		
479	launched by	
SS		
MS		
480	could not wait to	
SS		
MS		

481	extol the virtues of	
SS		
MS		
482	sought to	
SS		
MS		
483	showed up at	
SS		
MS		
484	enough for	
SS		
MS		
485	affected by	
SS		
MS		
486	earlier this month	
SS		
MS		

487	there needs to be	
SS		
MS		
488	extraneous details	
SS		
MS		
489	put the onus on	
SS		
MS		
490	crisis actors	
SS		
MS		
491	totally under	
SS		
MS		
492	got a pass on	
SS		
MS		

493	what bothers me	
SS		
MS		
494	got pushed off	
SS		
MS		
495	openly mock (someone)	
SS		
MS		
496	so dispirited that	
SS		
MS		
497	pointing fingers at	
SS		
MS		
498	part and parcel of	
SS		
MS		

499	countered by	
SS		
MS		
500	exulted in	
SS		
MS		
501	ad boycott	
SS		
MS		
502	take a hit	
SS		
MS		
503	has an effect on	
SS		
MS		
504	utterly remarkable	
SS		
MS		

505	no indication that	
SS		
MS		
506	two-pronged investigation	
SS		
MS		
507	multiple issues	
SS		
MS		
508	concocted a story	
SS		
MS		
509	a remarkable tweetstorm	
SS		
MS		
510	an unsolved mystery	
SS		
MS		

511	a microcosm of	
SS		
MS		
512	try and examine	
SS		
MS		
513	no prior warning	
SS		
MS		
514	true to life	
SS		
MS		
515	play-by-play account	
SS		
MS		
516	saw the writing on the wall	
SS		
MS		

517	fabricated evidence	
SS		
MS		
518	bursting at the seams	
SS		
MS		
519	yes men and women	
SS		
MS		
520	very eagerly	
SS		
MS		
521	bland response	
SS		
MS		
522	refused to admit	
SS		
MS		

523	chop it up with	
SS		
MS		
524	in usable form	
SS		
MS		
525	the final word	
SS		
MS		
526	against the idea	
SS		
MS		
527	elaborate on	
SS		
MS		
528	attempt to dislodge	
SS		
MS		

529	went to unusual lengths to	
SS		
MS		
530	cowed by	
SS		
MS		
531	can't comment	
SS		
MS		
532	no legitimate reason	
SS		
MS		
533	weekly reports	
SS		
MS		
534	become more dire	
SS		
MS		

535	only half right	
SS		
MS		
536	an unsubstantiated rumor	
SS		
MS		
537	a body double	
SS		
MS		
538	preserve the facade	
SS		
MS		
539	a facile explanation	
SS		
MS		
540	rumor has it that	
SS		
MS		

541	wreak havoc	
SS		
MS		
542	crazy stories	
SS		
MS		
543	twist (oneself) into a pretzel to	
SS		
MS		
544	a stain on	
SS		
MS		
545	simply trying to	
SS		
MS		
546	suffer without redress	
SS		
MS		

547	conducted an investigation	
SS		
MS		
548	several occasions	
SS		
MS		
549	have nothing against	
SS		
MS		
550	it's uncommon for	
SS		
MS		
551	a stark example of	
SS		
MS		
552	absolutely wrong	
SS		
MS		

553	take the first step	
SS		
MS		
554	a litany of	
SS		
MS		
555	my warmest sympathy goes out to	
SS		
MS		
556	the latest request from	
SS		
MS		
557	take-home pay	
SS		
MS		
558	reaction to	
SS		
MS		

559	strike fear into	
SS		
MS		
560	on pins and needles	
SS		
MS		
561	expected to succeed	
SS		
MS		
562	repeatedly condemned	
SS		
MS		
563	acted as though	
SS		
MS		
564	so appalling	
SS		
MS		

565	seen an increase in	
SS		
MS		
566	an unmistakable increase	
SS		
MS		
567	other kinds of	
SS		
MS		
568	belies the facts	
SS		
MS		
569	completely ridiculous	
SS		
MS		
570	a small group of	
SS		
MS		

571	rising threat	
SS		
MS		
572	the entire landscape of	
SS		
MS		
573	extremely fortunate	
SS		
MS		
574	stand back	
SS		
MS		
575	much more important	
SS		
MS		
576	spent an ungodly sum of money	
SS		
MS		

577	book a hotel	
SS		
MS		
578	just how easy	
SS		
MS		
579	impressive to	
SS		
MS		
580	fallacious arguments	
SS		
MS		
581	freaked out about	
SS		
MS		
582	ritzy dinner	
SS		
MS		

583	an unparalleled chance	
SS		
MS		
584	fastidious about	
SS		
MS		
585	paid for by	
SS		
MS		
586	an act of defiance	
SS		
MS		
587	a legal decision	
SS		
MS		
588	wind gusts	
SS		
MS		

589	punishing blizzard conditions	
SS		
MS		
590	a triple threat	
SS		
MS		
591	delay the decision	
SS		
MS		
592	a barrage of	
SS		
MS		
593	a human chain	
SS		
MS		
594	significant escalation	
SS		
MS		

595	coursing through	
SS		
MS		
596	draw the connection	
SS		
MS		
597	act upon	
SS		
MS		
598	so struck by	
SS		
MS		
599	an overt threat	
SS		
MS		
600	a veiled threat	
SS		
MS		

601	couldn't fathom	
SS		
MS		
602	digital footprint	
SS		
MS		
603	a conversation about	
SS		
MS		
604	complementary to	
SS		
MS		
605	around the country	
SS		
MS		
606	directed people to	
SS		
MS		

607	fatuous notions	
SS		
MS		
608	because of the gravity of	
SS		
MS		
609	hard to absorb	
SS		
MS		
610	took place in	
SS		
MS		
611	a great relationship	
SS		
MS		
612	sincere intention	
SS		
MS		

613	dangling the possibility of	
SS		
MS		
614	terror attack	
SS		
MS		
615	strong condemnation	
SS		
MS		
616	feel very frightened	
SS		
MS		
617	a zero-sum game	
SS		
MS		
618	started a petition	
SS		
MS		

619	happily accept being	
SS		
MS		
620	brought up in	
SS		
MS		
621	fecund fields	
SS		
MS		
622	very foreign	
SS		
MS		
623	family-oriented people	
SS		
MS		
624	felt alive	
SS		
MS		

625	sufficient destructive power	
SS		
MS		
626	marvel at	
SS		
MS		
627	in turmoil	
SS		
MS		
628	consider the possibility	
SS		
MS		
629	taunted by	
SS		
MS		
630	getting desperate	
SS		
MS		

631	Friday night	
SS		
MS		
632	with military precision	
SS		
MS		
633	automatic device	
SS		
MS		
634	murky details	
SS		
MS		
635	just don't understand	
SS		
MS		
636	for civilians	
SS		
MS		

637	get to decide	
SS		
MS		
638	the beginning of the end	
SS		
MS		
639	pull back the mask on	
SS		
MS		
640	a futile approach	
SS		
MS		
641	may have become	
SS		
MS		
642	took no action	
SS		
MS		

643	suss out	
SS		
MS		
644	in waiting	
SS		
MS		
645	felicitous weather	
SS		
MS		
646	no shortage of	
SS		
MS		
647	long journey	
SS		
MS		
648	told an untruth	
SS		
MS		

649	feral cats	
SS		
MS		
650	one or more	
SS		
MS		
651	a sad conclusion to	
SS		
MS		
652	under oath	
SS		
MS		
653	nothing further to add	
SS		
MS		
654	appears to be saying	
SS		
MS		

655	an unfair assessment	
SS		
MS		
656	within minutes of	
SS		
MS		
657	fervent prayer	
SS		
MS		
658	the timing of	
SS		
MS		
659	doesn't fit	
SS		
MS		
660	down the road	
SS		
MS		

661	the next station	
SS		
MS		
662	conceded that	
SS		
MS		
663	opening statement	
SS		
MS		
664	explain why	
SS		
MS		
665	enter the race	
SS		
MS		
666	mentioned that	
SS		
MS		

667	did not deny	
SS		
MS		
668	bobbing and weaving	
SS		
MS		
669	pull the door handle	
SS		
MS		
670	growing nervousness	
SS		
MS		
671	welcoming to	
SS		
MS		
672	very endearing	
SS		
MS		

673	pass along	
SS		
MS		
674	why go through	
SS		
MS		
675	set up for disappointment	
SS		
MS		
676	a great disservice to	
SS		
MS		
677	there is a chance to	
SS		
MS		
678	there is a chance for	
SS		
MS		

679	the proof of	
SS		
MS		
680	acceptable behavior	
SS		
MS		
681	told not to	
SS		
MS		
682	for deceptive purposes	
SS		
MS		
683	factually incorrect	
SS		
MS		
684	makes more clear than ever	
SS		
MS		

685	there's no clear favorite	
SS		
MS		
686	obviously aware	
SS		
MS		
687	fly in the face of	
SS		
MS		
688	appears to be	
SS		
MS		
689	thread the needle	
SS		
MS		
690	a canny person	
SS		
MS		

691	quipped about	
SS		
MS		
692	just this morning	
SS		
MS		
693	a fatal accident	
SS		
MS		
694	cozy relationship	
SS		
MS		
695	deep ties to	
SS		
MS		
696	to no avail	
SS		
MS		

697	one of the worst	
SS		
MS		
698	open an inquiry into	
SS		
MS		
699	out of an abundance of caution	
SS		
MS		
700	a moment of serenity	
SS		
MS		
701	a very serious decision	
SS		
MS		
702	an audience of one	
SS		
MS		

703	a big chunk of time	
SS		
MS		
704	why else would	
SS		
MS		
705	fetid odour	
SS		
MS		
706	fettered by	
SS		
MS		
707	completely at odds	
SS		
MS		
708	exercise discretion	
SS		
MS		

709	fickle weather	
SS		
MS		
710	split the difference	
SS		
MS		
711	less than an hour after	
SS		
MS		
712	a formidable candidate	
SS		
MS		
713	drowned out	
SS		
MS		
714	a lot of enthusiasm	
SS		
MS		

715	fidelity to	
SS		
MS		
716	on the up and up	
SS		
MS		
717	doesn't deserve	
SS		
MS		
718	crowded field	
SS		
MS		
719	went from bad to worse	
SS		
MS		
720	resist the urge to	
SS		
MS		

721	figurative language	
SS		
MS		
722	in the midst of	
SS		
MS		
723	insanely cool	
SS		
MS		
724	a crushing blow	
SS		
MS		
725	get a fair trial	
SS		
MS		
726	unsavory people	
SS		
MS		

727	flabbergasted by	
SS		
MS		
728	several weeks ago	
SS		
MS		
729	a huge breach	
SS		
MS		
730	sent shock waves through	
SS		
MS		
731	completely improper	
SS		
MS		
732	not enough time	
SS		
MS		

733	a flaccid handshake	
SS		
MS		
734	expressed disgust for	
SS		
MS		
735	a long career	
SS		
MS		
736	take a personal jab at	
SS		
MS		
737	backed down from	
SS		
MS		
738	a booming economy	
SS		
MS		

739	a flagrant abuse of	
SS		
MS		
740	to make sure that	
SS		
MS		
741	appropriate measures	
SS		
MS		
742	hang out with	
SS		
MS		
743	so predictable	
SS		
MS		
744	pretend to be	
SS		
MS		

745	not charged	
SS		
MS		
746	a florid complexion	
SS		
MS		
747	did not immediately respond to	
SS		
MS		
748	as purported	
SS		
MS		
749	a doctored photo	
SS		
MS		
750	get expelled	
SS		
MS		

751	from ancient days	
SS		
MS		
752	flouted authority	
SS		
MS		
753	across the front	
SS		
MS		
754	knowledge sharing	
SS		
MS		
755	must listen to	
SS		
MS		
756	did not acknowledge	
SS		
MS		

757	foiled by	
SS		
MS		
758	demand access to	
SS		
MS		
759	forced removal of	
SS		
MS		
760	has not followed	
SS		
MS		
761	a bitter contest	
SS		
MS		
762	gained access to	
SS		
MS		

763	foraged for	
SS		
MS		
764	used to assss whether	
SS		
MS		
765	without consent	
SS		
MS		
766	at much higher rates	
SS		
MS		
767	went missing	
SS		
MS		
768	a shameful history	
SS		
MS		

769	showed forbearance	
SS		
MS		
770	bitter conflict	
SS		
MS		
771	grow more important	
SS		
MS		
772	it usually takes many years	
SS		
MS		
773	wrote extensively	
SS		
MS		
774	when all else fails	
SS		
MS		

775	forestalled criticism	
SS		
MS		
776	largely reliant on	
SS		
MS		
777	stretches across	
SS		
MS		
778	one of only a few	
SS		
MS		
779	a good response to	
SS		
MS		
780	during the daytime	
SS		
MS		

781	a forlorn landscape	
SS		
MS		
782	very destructive to	
SS		
MS		
783	in daily communication with	
SS		
MS		
784	before the advent of	
SS		
MS		
785	the most reliable way	
SS		
MS		
786	exchange personal messages	
SS		
MS		

787	low volume	
SS		
MS		
788	likely to happen	
SS		
MS		
789	in today's climate	
SS		
MS		
790	combined with	
SS		
MS		
791	reduce cost	
SS		
MS		
792	singled out by	
SS		
MS		

793	forsake A for B	
SS		
MS		
794	compete for	
SS		
MS		
795	as far as I can tell	
SS		
MS		
796	strongly prefer to	
SS		
MS		
797	consider for a moment	
SS		
MS		
798	ride pillion	
SS		
MS		

799	intestinal fortitude	
SS		
MS		
800	to no one's surprise	
SS		
MS		
801	failed to create	
SS		
MS		
802	throughout most of	
SS		
MS		
803	existed long before	
SS		
MS		
804	swirl around	
SS		
MS		

805	too small a market to	
SS		
MS		
806	with the possible exception of	
SS		
MS		
807	a symbol of	
SS		
MS		
808	it's no surprise	
SS		
MS		
809	ranks well above	
SS		
MS		
810	a huge priority for	
SS		
MS		

811	a fortuitous circumstance	
SS		
MS		
812	cut down on	
SS		
MS		
813	as a last resort	
SS		
MS		
814	from infancy through to	
SS		
MS		
815	the continuity of	
SS		
MS		
816	due to limited space	
SS		
MS		

817	transferred from	
SS		
MS		
818	late last year	
SS		
MS		
819	in foster care	
SS		
MS		
820	working with	
SS		
MS		
821	youth services	
SS		
MS		
822	a forum for	
SS		
MS		

823	foster a sense of	
SS		
MS		
824	a fractious relationship	
SS		
MS		
825	fraught with	
SS		
MS		
826	frenetic pace	
SS		
MS		
827	frivolous activity	
SS		
MS		
828	a frugal shopper	
SS		
MS		

829	a furtive glance	
SS		
MS		
830	casual employment	
SS		
MS		
831	a stable job	
SS		
MS		
832	bring a message of	
SS		
MS		
833	named in honour of	
SS		
MS		
834	weekend tournament	
SS		
MS		

835	made an exceptional contribution to	
SS		
MS		
836	a garish display	
SS		
MS		
837	the next recipient of	
SS		
MS		
838	can't commit to	
SS		
MS		
839	jurisdiction over	
SS		
MS		
840	jump to the conclusion that	
SS		
MS		

841	more garrulous than	
SS		
MS		
842	presented in	
SS		
MS		
843	raise funds for	
SS		
MS		
844	set to launch on	
SS		
MS		
845	scurrilous accusations	
SS		
MS		
846	extradition of	
SS		
MS		

847	a genial host	
SS		
MS		
848	go into effect	
SS		
MS		
849	city council meeting	
SS		
MS		
850	will be appointed	
SS		
MS		
851	shrouded in secrecy	
SS		
MS		
852	crashed into	
SS		
MS		

853	found common cause with	
SS		
MS		
854	from the get-go	
SS		
MS		
855	reasonably sober	
SS		
MS		
856	criticism directed at	
SS		
MS		
857	current role	
SS		
MS		
858	took heat for	
SS		
MS		

859	glutton for punishment	
SS		
MS		
860	a lifetime position	
SS		
MS		
861	hatred for	
SS		
MS		
862	drew a mixed reaction	
SS		
MS		
863	deadly crash	
SS		
MS		
864	minutes after	
SS		
MS		

865	goaded on by	
SS		
MS		
866	rising waters	
SS		
MS		
867	a fecund source of	
SS		
MS		
868	serious hazards	
SS		
MS		
869	deprive X of	
SS		
MS		
870	out of sight	
SS		
MS		

871	a gourmand's paradise	
SS		
MS		
872	impossible to pay off	
SS		
MS		
873	pay off a debt	
SS		
MS		
874	there doesn't need to be	
SS		
MS		
875	cannot leave	
SS		
MS		
876	worth around	
SS		
MS		

877	difficult to know for sure	
SS		
MS		
878	the consent of	
SS		
MS		
879	grandiloquent language	
SS		
MS		
880	at any time in history	
SS		
MS		
881	it's thought that there are	
SS		
MS		
882	meticulous about	
SS		
MS		

883	report on	
SS		
MS		
884	come to light	
SS		
MS		
885	new information	
SS		
MS		
886	will not hesitate to	
SS		
MS		
887	victimized by	
SS		
MS		
888	divided on whether	
SS		
MS		

889	last-ditch effort	
SS		
MS		
890	the exact cause	
SS		
MS		
891	in the meantime	
SS		
MS		
892	cross a threshold	
SS		
MS		
893	ground the airplane	
SS		
MS		
894	would no longer allow	
SS		
MS		

895	did not have prior knowledge of	
SS		
MS		
896	grandiose plans	
SS		
MS		
897	on board	
SS		
MS		
898	asked to return to	
SS		
MS		
899	plummeted into	
SS		
MS		
900	in the country	
SS		
MS		

901	gratuitous violence	
SS		
MS		
902	the safety of	
SS		
MS		
903	the possibility of	
SS		
MS		
904	identified similarities between A and B	
SS		
MS		
905	similarities between	
SS		
MS		
906	lost control of	
SS		
MS		

907	a gregarious personality	
SS		
MS		
908	stole (something) from	
SS		
MS		
909	give a boost to	
SS		
MS		
910	there's no justification for	
SS		
MS		
911	aren't accessible to	
SS		
MS		
912	recruited to	
SS		
MS		

913	benefit from	
SS		
MS		
914	at every turn	
SS		
MS		
915	grievous injury	
SS		
MS		
916	in leaps and bounds	
SS		
MS		
917	take a spot away from	
SS		
MS		
918	hit a nerve	
SS		
MS		

919	resorted to guile	
SS		
MS		
920	not entirely wrong	
SS		
MS		
921	just how much	
SS		
MS		
922	the advantages of	
SS		
MS		
923	intended to help	
SS		
MS		
924	factors such as	
SS		
MS		

925	hackneyed joke	
SS		
MS		
926	spurred discussions	
SS		
MS		
927	come to realize that	
SS		
MS		
928	guilty conscience	
SS		
MS		
929	put together	
SS		
MS		
930	got X to	
SS		
MS		

931	a disturbing incident	
SS		
MS		
932	not sure if	
SS		
MS		
933	a funeral service	
SS		
MS		
934	well travelled	
SS		
MS		
935	widely seen as	
SS		
MS		
936	change jobs	
SS		
MS		

937	by midnight	
SS		
MS		
938	on the tarmac	
SS		
MS		
939	an inconvenience to	
SS		
MS		
940	why it took so long	
SS		
MS		
941	welcomed the decision to	
SS		
MS		
942	air concerns over	
SS		
MS		

943	hallowed ground	
SS		
MS		
944	hours after	
SS		
MS		
945	cracked down on	
SS		
MS		
946	roamed the halls of	
SS		
MS		
947	it didn't take long before	
SS		
MS		
948	on the spectrum	
SS		
MS		

949	harangued about	
SS		
MS		
950	started running	
SS		
MS		
951	hardy plants	
SS		
MS		
952	gathered outside	
SS		
MS		
953	determine how	
SS		
MS		
954	stopped going to	
SS		
MS		

955	harrowing ordeal	
SS		
MS		
956	embrace a message of	
SS		
MS		
957	withering criticism	
SS		
MS		
958	a daily battle to	
SS		
MS		
959	the entrance of	
SS		
MS		
960	will continue despite	
SS		
MS		

961	a haughty attitude	
SS		
MS		
962	media savvy	
SS		
MS		
963	sent a text message	
SS		
MS		
964	the victim of	
SS		
MS		
965	despite the fact that	
SS		
MS		
966	illegal activity	
SS		
MS		

967	quite a hedonist	
SS		
MS		
968	granted approval	
SS		
MS		
969	correct the answers	
SS		
MS		
970	admission to	
SS		
MS		
971	a game plan	
SS		
MS		
972	if ever asked	
SS		
MS		

973	hold fast to	
SS		
MS		
974	made arrangements to	
SS		
MS		
975	very frequently	
SS		
MS		
976	a side door	
SS		
MS		
977	hegemony	
SS		
MS		
978	conspired with	
SS		
MS		

979	heinous crime	
SS		
MS		
980	a business owner	
SS		
MS		
981	asked to explain	
SS		
MS		
982	under scrutiny	
SS		
MS		
983	government service	
SS		
MS		
984	as arduous as	
SS		
MS		

985	a lack of experience	
SS		
MS		
986	heterogeneous classrooms	
SS		
MS		
987	it is hugely important	
SS		
MS		
988	a tough cookie	
SS		
MS		
989	money laundering	
SS		
MS		
990	would be much better off	
SS		
MS		

991	cherished ideals	
SS		
MS		
992	hint at	
SS		
MS		
993	a short hiatus	
SS		
MS		
994	revive the question of	
SS		
MS		
995	find it almost impossible to	
SS		
MS		
996	it's easy to forget that	
SS		
MS		

997	so prevalent	
SS		
MS		
998	company hierarchy	
SS		
MS		
999	spiralled into	
SS		
MS		
1,000	actual skill	
SS		
MS		
1,001	runs completely counter to	
SS		
MS		
1,002	an internal investigation	
SS		
MS		

1,003	go to great lengths	
SS		
MS		
1,004	the hypocrisy of	
SS		
MS		
1,005	call time on (something)	
SS		
MS		
1,006	there's plenty to criticize about	
SS		
MS		
1,007	hypothetical matchup	
SS		
MS		
1,008	willing to tell the truth	
SS		
MS		

1,009	an iconoclast	
SS		
MS		
1,010	dig deeper	
SS		
MS		
1,011	get favor from	
SS		
MS		
1,012	spew out	
SS		
MS		
1,013	a false story	
SS		
MS		
1,014	legally bound to	
SS		
MS		

1,015	over and over again	
SS		
MS		
1,016	shovel snow	
SS		
MS		
1,017	not involved in	
SS		
MS		
1,018	scraping by	
SS		
MS		
1,019	in a tight race	
SS		
MS		
1,020	much more likely	
SS		
MS		

1,021	idiosyncratic merchants	
SS		
MS		
1,022	apt to	
SS		
MS		
1,023	have connections to	
SS		
MS		
1,024	try to tease out	
SS		
MS		
1,025	old enough to	
SS		
MS		
1,026	has little to do with	
SS		
MS		

1,027	considered idolatrous	
SS		
MS		
1,028	with access to	
SS		
MS		
1,029	it's absurd to	
SS		
MS		
1,030	wasn't appropriate	
SS		
MS		
1,031	in a variety of	
SS		
MS		
1,032	a degraded world	
SS		
MS		

1,033	ignominious result	
SS		
MS		
1,034	a narrow-minded thinker	
SS		
MS		
1,035	twice as fast	
SS		
MS		
1,036	illicit drugs	
SS		
MS		
1,037	a focal point	
SS		
MS		
1,038	right a wrong	
SS		
MS		

1,039	immerse (oneself) in	
SS		
MS		
1,040	not get sidetracked	
SS		
MS		
1,041	an ongoing process	
SS		
MS		
1,042	imitated by	
SS		
MS		
1,043	not a pipe dream	
SS		
MS		
1,044	reduced productivity	
SS		
MS		

1,045	immutable laws	
SS		
MS		
1,046	got sticker shock	
SS		
MS		
1,047	cross (one's) t's and dot (one's) i's	
SS		
MS		
1,048	in the most incredible way	
SS		
MS		
1,049	pleasantly surprised	
SS		
MS		
1,050	felt real	
SS		
MS		

1,051	an impassive observer	
SS		
MS		
1,052	highly stressful	
SS		
MS		
1,053	feel authentic	
SS		
MS		
1,054	going through	
SS		
MS		
1,055	give (something) a go	
SS		
MS		
1,056	stuck on	
SS		
MS		

1,057	speaks impeccable English	
SS		
MS		
1,058	such a big fan	
SS		
MS		
1,059	wants to announce	
SS		
MS		
1,060	nothing is as distracting as	
SS		
MS		
1,061	can't have it both ways	
SS		
MS		
1,062	in the rush	
SS		
MS		

1,063	impecunious adjunct professor	
SS		
MS		
1,064	take a step back	
SS		
MS		
1,065	decided willy-nilly to	
SS		
MS		
1,066	it's humorous that	
SS		
MS		
1,067	a private citizen	
SS		
MS		
1,068	unnamed sources	
SS		
MS		

1,069	it is imperative that	
SS		
MS		
1,070	simply does not exist	
SS		
MS		
1,071	could not be more proud	
SS		
MS		
1,072	made no sense	
SS		
MS		
1,073	highly contested	
SS		
MS		
1,074	painful process	
SS		
MS		

1,075	a viable counteroffer	
SS		
MS		
1,076	might have talked	
SS		
MS		
1,077	never instructed	
SS		
MS		
1,078	incendiary statements	
SS		
MS		
1,079	flagrant disregard	
SS		
MS		
1,080	weight in on	
SS		
MS		

1,081	so secretive about	
SS		
MS		
1,082	foreign policy	
SS		
MS		
1,083	a special case	
SS		
MS		
1,084	deserves to know	
SS		
MS		
1,085	written remarks	
SS		
MS		
1,086	iron-clad commitment	
SS		
MS		

1,087	raised questions about	
SS		
MS		
1,088	win over	
SS		
MS		
1,089	a top-line point	
SS		
MS		
1,090	consistent with	
SS		
MS		
1,091	no hard and fast rules	
SS		
MS		
1,092	full-throated denial	
SS		
MS		

1,093	considering the possibility	
SS		
MS		
1,094	disparaging of	
SS		
MS		
1,095	take the steam out of	
SS		
MS		
1,096	lay a marker with	
SS		
MS		
1,097	try to verify	
SS		
MS		
1,098	in full swing	
SS		
MS		

1,099	in total agreement with	
SS		
MS		
1,100	on everybody's lips	
SS		
MS		
1,101	budge a little bit	
SS		
MS		
1,102	have the upper hand	
SS		
MS		
1,103	like nailing jello to the wall	
SS		
MS		
1,104	partly blame	
SS		
MS		

1,105	partly to blame	
SS		
MS		
1,106	opened a probe into	
SS		
MS		
1,107	florid writing	
SS		
MS		
1,108	slept through	
SS		
MS		
1,109	pave a ne road	
SS		
MS		
1,110	throw cold water on	
SS		
MS		

1,111	an imperious manner	
SS		
MS		
1,112	impertinent questions	
SS		
MS		
1,113	wishful thinking	
SS		
MS		
1,114	would not knowingly meet	
SS		
MS		
1,115	the person with whom	
SS		
MS		
1,116	a friend of min	
SS		
MS		

1,117	impervious to	
SS		
MS		
1,118	not a spring chicken	
SS		
MS		
1,119	pored over	
SS		
MS		
1,120	would have sufficed	
SS		
MS		
1,121	a crowded field	
SS		
MS		
1,122	the key point	
SS		
MS		

1,123	an impetuous decision	
SS		
MS		
1,124	intensive care	
SS		
MS		
1,125	get so petty	
SS		
MS		
1,126	can't get into	
SS		
MS		
1,127	a lot of documents	
SS		
MS		
1,128	there could be	
SS		
MS		

1,129	impinges upon	
SS		
MS		
1,130	align (one's) with	
SS		
MS		
1,131	there's no way that	
SS		
MS		
1,132	seek leniency	
SS		
MS		
1,133	the department of justice	
SS		
MS		
1,134	look into	
SS		
MS		

1,135	implacable hatred	
SS		
MS		
1,136	farming implements	
SS		
MS		
1,137	need corroboration	
SS		
MS		
1,138	have credibility issues	
SS		
MS		
1,139	personally asked	
SS		
MS		
1,140	decision making	
SS		
MS		

1,141	growing concerns	
SS		
MS		
1,142	fine people	
SS		
MS		
1,143	soured on	
SS		
MS		
1,144	sparked by	
SS		
MS		
1,145	with valour	
SS		
MS		
1,146	to avoid any	
SS		
MS		

1,147	implicated in	
SS		
MS		
1,148	it sure seems like	
SS		
MS		
1,149	trying to profit from	
SS		
MS		
1,150	definitely knew	
SS		
MS		
1,151	one of the top three	
SS		
MS		
1,152	environmentally conscious	
SS		
MS		

1,153	implicit in	
SS		
MS		
1,154	rank highly on	
SS		
MS		
1,155	a vigorous approach	
SS		
MS		
1,156	very touching	
SS		
MS		
1,157	undue influence	
SS		
MS		
1,158	I for one	
SS		
MS		

1,159	impregnable fortress	
SS		
MS		
1,160	important because	
SS		
MS		
1,161	attributed to	
SS		
MS		
1,162	from the inception of	
SS		
MS		
1,163	hit some roadblocks	
SS		
MS		
1,164	move mountains	
SS		
MS		

1,165	impudent behaviour	
SS		
MS		
1,166	so different from	
SS		
MS		
1,167	a place to	
SS		
MS		
1,168	a sombre start	
SS		
MS		
1,169	a decade of hope	
SS		
MS		
1,170	noted for	
SS		
MS		

1,171	can be used to	
SS		
MS		
1,172	under suspicious circumstances	
SS		
MS		
1,173	expressed disappointment when	
SS		
MS		
1,174	an angry retort	
SS		
MS		
1,175	far from the truth	
SS		
MS		
1,176	the noonday sun	
SS		
MS		

1,177	imputed the errors to	
SS		
MS		
1,178	with a reputation as	
SS		
MS		
1,179	a fleeting urge to	
SS		
MS		
1,180	not always visible from	
SS		
MS		
1,181	refused to allow	
SS		
MS		
1,182	repeatedly interrupted	
SS		
MS		

1,183	inane comments	
SS		
MS		
1,184	paid careful attention to	
SS		
MS		
1,185	very much to the point	
SS		
MS		
1,186	stayed out of	
SS		
MS		
1,187	all the while	
SS		
MS		
1,188	a breakneck pace	
SS		
MS		

1,189	somewhat inarticulate	
SS		
MS		
1,190	fend for	
SS		
MS		
1,191	swear allegiance to	
SS		
MS		
1,192	resisted pressure to	
SS		
MS		
1,193	stopped short of saying	
SS		
MS		
1,194	a threat to	
SS		
MS		

1,195	incarnated in	
SS		
MS		
1,196	makes clear that	
SS		
MS		
1,197	wrestling with how to	
SS		
MS		
1,198	asked to come	
SS		
MS		
1,199	hundreds of people	
SS		
MS		
1,200	spend far more	
SS		
MS		

1,201	incendiary comment	
SS		
MS		
1,202	driven out of	
SS		
MS		
1,203	surprised at	
SS		
MS		
1,204	criminal investigation	
SS		
MS		
1,205	as many as	
SS		
MS		
1,206	in government	
SS		
MS		

1,207	grilled by	
SS		
MS		
1,208	a major story	
SS		
MS		
1,209	never purposely	
SS		
MS		
1,210	absolutely irate over	
SS		
MS		
1,211	questions arise about	
SS		
MS		
1,212	got teary	
SS		
MS		

1,213	incessant carping	
SS		
MS		
1,214	committed a serious crime	
SS		
MS		
1,215	made a choice	
SS		
MS		
1,216	far more lenient than	
SS		
MS		
1,217	in shambles	
SS		
MS		
1,218	a gross understatement	
SS		
MS		

1,219	inchoate yearnings	
SS		
MS		
1,220	unforgivable act	
SS		
MS		
1,221	a day of reckoning	
SS		
MS		
1,222	stunning comments	
SS		
MS		
1,223	a great deal of leverage	
SS		
MS		
1,224	a bridge too far	
SS		
MS		

1,225	too far afield	
SS		
MS		
1,226	incisive remark	
SS		
MS		
1,227	what's (one's) take on	
SS		
MS		
1,228	perfectly within (one's) purview	
SS		
MS		
1,229	provide a motive for	
SS		
MS		
1,230	in increments of	
SS		
MS		

1,231	incumbent on	
SS		
MS		
1,232	on heightened alert	
SS		
MS		
1,233	confidence is shaken	
SS		
MS		
1,234	not entirely clear	
SS		
MS		
1,235	disparaging to	
SS		
MS		
1,236	pretty disturbing	
SS		
MS		

1,237	provide a motive	
SS		
MS		
1,238	after the interview	
SS		
MS		
1,239	rule (something) out	
SS		
MS		
1,240	free to talk about	
SS		
MS		
1,241	a breach of	
SS		
MS		
1,242	lay down a warning	
SS		
MS		

1,243	indefatigable patience	
SS		
MS		
1,244	feeling embarrassed	
SS		
MS		
1,245	unprecedented in history	
SS		
MS		
1,246	compelled to take action	
SS		
MS		
1,247	confidence is shaken	
SS		
MS		
1,248	strong bipartisan backlash	
SS		
MS		

1,249	dictate the boundaries of	
SS		
MS		
1,250	pretty disturbing	
SS		
MS		
1,251	came off the rails	
SS		
MS		
1,252	full-fledged	
SS		
MS		
1,253	tear down	
SS		
MS		
1,254	in the mainstream	
SS		
MS		

1,255	indigenous culture	
SS		
MS		
1,256	one of the things	
SS		
MS		
1,257	gave full flower to	
SS		
MS		
1,258	expressed faith in	
SS		
MS		
1,259	in a broader sense	
SS		
MS		
1,260	seemingly failed to	
SS		
MS		

1,261	blurred the lines	
SS		
MS		
1,262	a high-profile meeting	
SS		
MS		
1,263	indigent community	
SS		
MS		
1,264	go rogue	
SS		
MS		
1,265	the least likely	
SS		
MS		
1,266	may be starting to unravel	
SS		
MS		

1,267	expressed indignation at	
SS		
MS		
1,268	an indolent student	
SS		
MS		
1,269	a small footprint	
SS		
MS		
1,270	could be achieved by	
SS		
MS		
1,271	no empathy for	
SS		
MS		
1,272	a step-by-step approach	
SS		
MS		

1,273	indomitable spirit	
SS		
MS		
1,274	induce d by	
SS		
MS		
1,275	in the run-up to	
SS		
MS		
1,276	seek clarification from	
SS		
MS		
1,277	seek clarification on	
SS		
MS		
1,278	on both sides	
SS		
MS		

1,279	in the dark	
SS		
MS		
1,280	a convert to	
SS		
MS		
1,281	a merger between A and B	
SS		
MS		
1,282	inappropriate ties	
SS		
MS		
1,283	in my humble opinion	
SS		
MS		
1,284	completely in the clear	
SS		
MS		

1,285	end of the road	
SS		
MS		
1,286	directly involved	
SS		
MS		
1,287	already knew that	
SS		
MS		
1,288	it's not a question of whether	
SS		
MS		
1,289	approached by	
SS		
MS		
1,290	a critical day	
SS		
MS		

1,291	had no other choice but	
SS		
MS		
1,292	simply because	
SS		
MS		
1,293	extremely cooperating	
SS		
MS		
1,294	private session	
SS		
MS		
1,295	what I find astounding about X is…	
SS		
MS		
1,296	a direct question	
SS		
MS		

1,297	reached the point of	
SS		
MS		
1,298	how serious	
SS		
MS		
1,299	get along	
SS		
MS		
1,300	had suspicions about	
SS		
MS		
1,301	three weeks ago	
SS		
MS		
1,302	really good at	
SS		
MS		

1,303	the whole purpose of X was	
SS		
MS		
1,304	at the port of entry	
SS		
MS		
1,305	expressed condolences	
SS		
MS		
1,306	a feature, not a bug	
SS		
MS		
1,307	sense of accomplishment	
SS		
MS		
1,308	wouldn't mind being	
SS		
MS		

1,309	proven not to be	
SS		
MS		
1,310	inept at	
SS		
MS		
1,311	cause problems	
SS		
MS		
1,312	doubtful with	
SS		
MS		
1,313	don't need to	
SS		
MS		
1,314	sneak out	
SS		
MS		

1,315	infusion of	
SS		
MS		
1,316	obviously affected	
SS		
MS		
1,317	keep barrelling on	
SS		
MS		
1,318	began wildly gesticulating	
SS		
MS		
1,319	an ingenious device	
SS		
MS		
1,320	throughout the ordeal	
SS		
MS		

1,321	an ingenuous response	
SS		
MS		
1,322	comparable to	
SS		
MS		
1,323	break (one's) silence	
SS		
MS		
1,324	jarring news	
SS		
MS		
1,325	dared to	
SS		
MS		
1,326	lambasted for	
SS		
MS		

1,327	inhibited by	
SS		
MS		
1,328	the might of	
SS		
MS		
1,329	under the grip of	
SS		
MS		
1,330	under the control of	
SS		
MS		
1,331	remain in charge of	
SS		
MS		
1,332	provide X with	
SS		
MS		

1,333	inimical to	
SS		
MS		
1,334	pivoting to	
SS		
MS		
1,335	acquired the rights to	
SS		
MS		
1,336	very disappointed	
SS		
MS		
1,337	a standing invitation	
SS		
MS		
1,338	could not be released	
SS		
MS		

1,339	in a panic	
SS		
MS		
1,340	turn a blind eye to	
SS		
MS		
1,341	it's kind of foolish to	
SS		
MS		
1,342	reached out to	
SS		
MS		
1,343	an indispensable figure	
SS		
MS		
1,344	kept his composure	
SS		
MS		

1,345	a den of iniquity	
SS		
MS		
1,346	extremely professional	
SS		
MS		
1,347	did a fantastic job	
SS		
MS		
1,348	upset with	
SS		
MS		
1,349	so hard to believe	
SS		
MS		
1,350	grouse about	
SS		
MS		

1,351	an injunction against	
SS		
MS		
1,352	announced that	
SS		
MS		
1,353	didn't flinch from	
SS		
MS		
1,354	innate ability	
SS		
MS		
1,355	leaped up in anger	
SS		
MS		
1,356	drew praise on	
SS		
MS		

1,357	retract (one's) comments	
SS		
MS		
1,358	storm of protest	
SS		
MS		
1,359	the first chance	
SS		
MS		
1,360	loath to	
SS		
MS		
1,361	germane to	
SS		
MS		
1,362	a few months later	
SS		
MS		

1,363	an innocuous joke	
SS		
MS		
1,364	the whole time	
SS		
MS		
1,365	don't miss out on	
SS		
MS		
1,366	couldn't make out	
SS		
MS		
1,367	give advice	
SS		
MS		
1,368	braced against	
SS		
MS		

1,369	less straightforward than	
SS		
MS		
1,370	straighten up	
SS		
MS		
1,371	an innovative design	
SS		
MS		
1,372	at the kitchen table	
SS		
MS		
1,373	lean over	
SS		
MS		
1,374	annual ritual	
SS		
MS		

1,375	full of innuendo	
SS		
MS		
1,376	unsure now why	
SS		
MS		
1,377	was a long time coming	
SS		
MS		
1,378	hard at work	
SS		
MS		
1,379	scoop out	
SS		
MS		
1,380	determined to	
SS		
MS		

1,381	persistent inquisitor	
SS		
MS		
1,382	humbled by	
SS		
MS		
1,383	have to carry	
SS		
MS		
1,384	compete with	
SS		
MS		
1,385	felt a jab	
SS		
MS		
1,386	muffled voices	
SS		
MS		

1,387	insatiable appetite for	
SS		
MS		
1,388	make do with	
SS		
MS		
1,389	an insidious disease	
SS		
MS		
1,390	don't just want to	
SS		
MS		
1,391	most valuable to	
SS		
MS		
1,392	had high hopes for	
SS		
MS		

1,393	adequate funding	
SS		
MS		
1,394	an insipid movie	
SS		
MS		
1,395	insolent behaviour	
SS		
MS		
1,396	a convergence of	
SS		
MS		
1,397	on the path	
SS		
MS		
1,398	countless times	
SS		
MS		

1,399	insulated from	
SS		
MS		
1,400	head toward	
SS		
MS		
1,401	never stopped to	
SS		
MS		
1,402	an uptick in	
SS		
MS		
1,403	stand for	
SS		
MS		
1,404	because of	
SS		
MS		

1,405	afraid of	
SS		
MS		
1,406	never stop	
SS		
MS		
1,407	worked so hard	
SS		
MS		
1,408	it's totally okay to	
SS		
MS		
1,409	instead of	
SS		
MS		
1,410	take a closer look at	
SS		
MS		

1,411	instigated by	
SS		
MS		
1,412	having a hard time	
SS		
MS		
1,413	take stock of	
SS		
MS		
1,414	sits proudly at the head of	
SS		
MS		
1,415	in the future	
SS		
MS		
1,416	might be able to	
SS		
MS		

1,417	a hectic week	
SS		
MS		
1,418	get a sense of	
SS		
MS		
1,419	important to think about	
SS		
MS		
1,420	calmly respond to	
SS		
MS		
1,421	become more aware of	
SS		
MS		
1,422	unfairly critical of	
SS		
MS		

1,423	even though	
SS		
MS		
1,424	everybody from A to B	
SS		
MS		
1,425	insular world of	
SS		
MS		
1,426	make the situation better	
SS		
MS		
1,427	at risk of	
SS		
MS		
1,428	isn't very helpful	
SS		
MS		

1,429	yell at	
SS		
MS		
1,430	more than necessary	
SS		
MS		
1,431	in the long run	
SS		
MS		
1,432	take comfort in	
SS		
MS		
1,433	even while everybody was	
SS		
MS		
1,434	seized from	
SS		
MS		

1,435	an insurgent group	
SS		
MS		
1,436	it's totally okay	
SS		
MS		
1,437	effectively manage	
SS		
MS		
1,438	without even realizing	
SS		
MS		
1,439	on occasion	
SS		
MS		
1,440	too lofty	
SS		
MS		

1,441	try to set	
SS		
MS		
1,442	in pursuit of	
SS		
MS		
1,443	consider why	
SS		
MS		
1,444	the importance of	
SS		
MS		
1,445	woke up to	
SS		
MS		
1,446	pick up	
SS		
MS		

1,447	integral to	
SS		
MS		
1,448	help change	
SS		
MS		
1,449	step up the fight against	
SS		
MS		
1,450	strongly support	
SS		
MS		
1,451	may interject	
SS		
MS		
1,452	yet to be named	
SS		
MS		

1,453	challenged (one's) inter-locutors	
SS		
MS		
1,454	dump the program	
SS		
MS		
1,455	postpartum depression	
SS		
MS		
1,456	an interminable wait	
SS		
MS		
1,457	maternity care	
SS		
MS		
1,458	put a cap on	
SS		
MS		

1,459	an epigraph	
SS		
MS		
1,460	there is no evidence that	
SS		
MS		
1,461	the original plan	
SS		
MS		
1,462	intimations of	
SS		
MS		
1,463	does need work	
SS		
MS		
1,464	one wing of the party	
SS		
MS		

1,465	intractable problems	
SS		
MS		
1,466	struggling to quash	
SS		
MS		
1,467	intransigent	
SS		
MS		
1,468	talk (someone) out of an idea	
SS		
MS		
1,469	an intrepid adventurer	
SS		
MS		
1,470	inundated with	
SS		
MS		

1,471	back in the day	
SS		
MS		
1,472	bring up	
SS		
MS		
1,473	take a victory lap	
SS		
MS		
1,474	let (someone) off the hook	
SS		
MS		
1,475	inure X to	
SS		
MS		
1,476	mess up	
SS		
MS		

1,477	invective against	
SS		
MS		
1,478	so vital	
SS		
MS		
1,479	remonstrate with	
SS		
MS		
1,480	a game changer	
SS		
MS		
1,481	build resilience	
SS		
MS		
1,482	a normal part of	
SS		
MS		

1,483	lack of	
SS		
MS		
1,484	deserve answers on	
SS		
MS		
1,485	inviolable	
SS		
MS		
1,486	an irascible disposition	
SS		
MS		
1,487	exceedingly disagreeable	
SS		
MS		
1,488	ask about	
SS		
MS		

1,489	an iridescent gemstone	
SS		
MS		
1,490	a crazy moment	
SS		
MS		
1,491	express frustration	
SS		
MS		
1,492	strong opinions	
SS		
MS		
1,493	an irreverent sense of humour	
SS		
MS		
1,494	feel obligated	
SS		
MS		

1,495	completely inappropriate	
SS		
MS		
1,496	a jubilant celebration	
SS		
MS		
1,497	receive criticism	
SS		
MS		
1,498	can be devastating	
SS		
MS		
1,499	the latest example of	
SS		
MS		
1,500	have to deal with	
SS		
MS		

1,501	judicious use of	
SS		
MS		
1,502	not even allowed	
SS		
MS		
1,503	have high expectations	
SS		
MS		
1,504	good enough	
SS		
MS		
1,505	learn to solve	
SS		
MS		
1,506	most of the time	
SS		
MS		

1,507	grew up with	
SS		
MS		
1,508	aren't afraid to	
SS		
MS		
1,509	consistent complaints	
SS		
MS		
1,510	specialize in	
SS		
MS		
1,511	wariness about	
SS		
MS		
1,512	voice opposition to	
SS		
MS		

1,513	proper conversation	
SS		
MS		
1,514	tend to agree	
SS		
MS		
1,515	biggest worry	
SS		
MS		
1,516	pipe up and say	
SS		
MS		
1,517	not allowed to	
SS		
MS		
1,518	isn't an issue	
SS		
MS		

1,519	an irrevocable change	
SS		
MS		
1,520	chain of command	
SS		
MS		
1,521	keep it on the straight and narrow	
SS		
MS		
1,522	all indications are that	
SS		
MS		
1,523	doesn't always have to	
SS		
MS		
1,524	there is plenty of hope	
SS		
MS		

1,525	at the top of the hour	
SS		
MS		
1,526	in the lead-up to	
SS		
MS		
1,527	doesn't always have to be	
SS		
MS		
1,528	questionable evidence	
SS		
MS		
1,529	celebrity status	
SS		
MS		
1,530	looming deadline	
SS		
MS		

1,531	final salvo	
SS		
MS		
1,532	abject horror	
SS		
MS		
1,533	glued to	
SS		
MS		
1,534	course correction	
SS		
MS		
1,535	the juxtaposition of	
SS		
MS		
1,536	tend to agree	
SS		
MS		

1,537	death knell	
SS		
MS		
1,538	in moderation	
SS		
MS		
1,539	kudos to	
SS		
MS		
1,540	know how to	
SS		
MS		
1,541	suffered lacerations	
SS		
MS		
1,542	fixated on	
SS		
MS		

1,543	as enticing as	
SS		
MS		
1,544	a stable future	
SS		
MS		
1,545	constantly changing	
SS		
MS		
1,546	could see	
SS		
MS		
1,547	a laconic reply	
SS		
MS		
1,548	bundles of	
SS		
MS		

1,549	a languid pace	
SS		
MS		
1,550	plead guilty	
SS		
MS		
1,551	during the day	
SS		
MS		
1,552	has not been difficult	
SS		
MS		
1,553	tremendous desire to	
SS		
MS		
1,554	available for	
SS		
MS		

1,555	grand larceny	
SS		
MS		
1,556	a readiness to	
SS		
MS		
1,557	rushing water	
SS		
MS		
1,558	ongoing battle	
SS		
MS		
1,559	social interaction	
SS		
MS		
1,560	there's plenty of hope	
SS		
MS		

1,561	relied on the largesse of	
SS		
MS		
1,562	least surprising	
SS		
MS		
1,563	tout the success of	
SS		
MS		
1,564	believed to	
SS		
MS		
1,565	the use of	
SS		
MS		
1,566	disdain for	
SS		
MS		

1,567	a latent infection	
SS		
MS		
1,568	pulled together by	
SS		
MS		
1,569	no discernible outcome	
SS		
MS		
1,570	take the blame for	
SS		
MS		
1,571	more careful	
SS		
MS		
1,572	so happy that	
SS		
MS		

1,573	a laudatory review	
SS		
MS		
1,574	totally blindsided when	
SS		
MS		
1,575	was confident that	
SS		
MS		
1,576	fully prepared	
SS		
MS		
1,577	adoptive parent	
SS		
MS		
1,578	a good place to	
SS		
MS		

1,579	had to guess	
SS		
MS		
1,580	from the outset	
SS		
MS		
1,581	the only person who	
SS		
MS		
1,582	didn't use much	
SS		
MS		
1,583	very calm	
SS		
MS		
1,584	waiting by	
SS		
MS		

1,585	plan for	
SS		
MS		
1,586	a lavish donor	
SS		
MS		
1,587	too late	
SS		
MS		
1,588	rushed to	
SS		
MS		
1,589	an immense task	
SS		
MS		
1,590	faded from memory	
SS		
MS		

1,591	financial legerdemain	
SS		
MS		
1,592	the hardest part	
SS		
MS		
1,593	curry favour with	
SS		
MS		
1,594	not to mention	
SS		
MS		
1,595	puzzle through	
SS		
MS		
1,596	on the shortlist for	
SS		
MS		

1,597	a lenient sentence	
SS		
MS		
1,598	immensely helpful	
SS		
MS		
1,599	retreat to	
SS		
MS		
1,600	unable to	
SS		
MS		
1,601	less intimidating	
SS		
MS		
1,602	want to improve	
SS		
MS		

1,603	a truculent person	
SS		
MS		
1,604	created by	
SS		
MS		
1,605	a lethargic economy	
SS		
MS		
1,606	criminal liability	
SS		
MS		
1,607	bad reputation	
SS		
MS		
1,608	keep engaged with	
SS		
MS		

1,609	libertarian thinking	
SS		
MS		
1,610	found lots of ways to	
SS		
MS		
1,611	allows me to	
SS		
MS		
1,612	especially useful	
SS		
MS		
1,613	has the potential to	
SS		
MS		
1,614	what made me	
SS		
MS		

1,615	licentious behaviour	
SS		
MS		
1,616	silent on	
SS		
MS		
1,617	even when I feel	
SS		
MS		
1,618	it's so bad that	
SS		
MS		
1,619	increasingly affected	
SS		
MS		
1,620	in the past few years	
SS		
MS		

1,621	running through	
SS		
MS		
1,622	scrap plans to	
SS		
MS		
1,623	feel very isolated	
SS		
MS		
1,624	connect with	
SS		
MS		
1,625	fall short	
SS		
MS		
1,626	intended to tackle	
SS		
MS		

1,627	limpid prose	
SS		
MS		
1,628	a major problem	
SS		
MS		
1,629	completely contradict	
SS		
MS		
1,630	publicly apologize	
SS		
MS		
1,631	acknowledged that	
SS		
MS		
1,632	won the backing of	
SS		
MS		

1,633	the linchpin of	
SS		
MS		
1,634	kind of surprised by	
SS		
MS		
1,635	forced to perform	
SS		
MS		
1,636	find a position	
SS		
MS		
1,637	eventually return	
SS		
MS		
1,638	wanted to preserve	
SS		
MS		

1,639	lithe figure	
SS		
MS		
1,640	get sucked into	
SS		
MS		
1,641	serious pushback	
SS		
MS		
1,642	must endure	
SS		
MS		
1,643	became depressed	
SS		
MS		
1,644	must endure	
SS		
MS		

1,645	the litigants	
SS		
MS		
1,646	pick a fight with	
SS		
MS		
1,647	accurate information	
SS		
MS		
1,648	a great weekend	
SS		
MS		
1,649	lucid dreaming	
SS		
MS		
1,650	began working	
SS		
MS		

1,651	luminous eyes	
SS		
MS		
1,652	also known as	
SS		
MS		
1,653	lurid details	
SS		
MS		
1,654	catering to	
SS		
MS		
1,655	a huge believer in	
SS		
MS		
1,656	extremely grateful	
SS		
MS		

1,657	caught up in a maelstrom	
SS		
MS		
1,658	magnanimous gesture	
SS		
MS		
1,659	out of fear of	
SS		
MS		
1,660	unable to understand	
SS		
MS		
1,661	heaped malediction upon	
SS		
MS		
1,662	without concealing	
SS		
MS		

1,663	malevolent gossip	
SS		
MS		
1,664	can be a lot of fun	
SS		
MS		
1,665	didn't have the time to	
SS		
MS		
1,666	finally have the time to do	
SS		
MS		
1,667	stigma associated with	
SS		
MS		
1,668	in the media	
SS		
MS		

1,669	a malevolent lie	
SS		
MS		
1,670	an action junkie	
SS		
MS		
1,671	trips to	
SS		
MS		
1,672	a sacred mission	
SS		
MS		
1,653	not just about	
SS		
MS		
1,674	in collaboration with	
SS		
MS		

1,675	a malleable metal	
SS		
MS		
1,676	derive from	
SS		
MS		
1,677	earned praise	
SS		
MS		
1,678	in an array of	
SS		
MS		
1,679	almost daily	
SS		
MS		
1,680	decked out in	
SS		
MS		

1,681	given a mandate for	
SS		
MS		
1,682	attracted a huge following	
SS		
MS		
1,683	in front of	
SS		
MS		
1,684	doesn't seem to matter	
SS		
MS		
1,685	stand next to	
SS		
MS		
1,686	deal with	
SS		
MS		

1,687	manifested in	
SS		
MS		
1,688	able to respond to	
SS		
MS		
1,689	a full roster of	
SS		
MS		
1,690	hit the ground running	
SS		
MS		
1,691	manifold problems	
SS		
MS		
1,692	nothing of value	
SS		
MS		

1,693	maudlin poetry	
SS		
MS		
1,694	willingly pay	
SS		
MS		
1,695	did not appear	
SS		
MS		
1,696	feel joyous	
SS		
MS		
1,697	only when	
SS		
MS		
1,698	the same trend	
SS		
MS		

1,699	a bit of a maverick	
SS		
MS		
1,700	so over the top	
SS		
MS		
1,701	vary widely	
SS		
MS		
1,702	in part because	
SS		
MS		
1,703	fees for	
SS		
MS		
1,704	littered with	
SS		
MS		

1,705	mawkish movie	
SS		
MS		
1,706	favourite maxim	
SS		
MS		
1,707	seems implausible	
SS		
MS		
1,708	quickly forgotten	
SS		
MS		
1,709	quickly detrmined that	
SS		
MS		
1,710	doesn't affect	
SS		
MS		

1,711	a meagre breakfast	
SS		
MS		
1,712	lost touch	
SS		
MS		
1,713	a wider view of	
SS		
MS		
1,714	haven't heard	
SS		
MS		
1,715	made a splash	
SS		
MS		
1,716	it gives me great pleasure	
SS		
MS		

1,717	a 200-meter medley	
SS		
MS		
1,718	didn't seem to	
SS		
MS		
1,719	welcomed into	
SS		
MS		
1,720	got to know	
SS		
MS		
1,721	continued to	
SS		
MS		
1,722	became deeper	
SS		
MS		

1,723	a mendacious leader	
SS		
MS		
1,724	continued writing	
SS		
MS		
1,725	never get to	
SS		
MS		
1,726	a good opportunity to	
SS		
MS		
1,727	hit it off	
SS		
MS		
1,728	in no uncertain terms	
SS		
MS		

1,729	mercurial wit	
SS		
MS		
1,730	direct orders	
SS		
MS		
1,731	three years running	
SS		
MS		
1,732	decided to	
SS		
MS		
1,733	given a heads-up	
SS		
MS		
1,734	for a time	
SS		
MS		

1,735	made a tremendous difference	
SS		
MS		
1,736	wasn't particularly good at	
SS		
MS		
1,737	the aim of X is to ensure that	
SS		
MS		
1,738	very proud to	
SS		
MS		
1,739	hopped up on	
SS		
MS		
1,740	an amazing initiative	
SS		
MS		

1,741	keep meticulous records	
SS		
MS		
1,742	benefit from	
SS		
MS		
1,743	beginning to understand that	
SS		
MS		
1,744	as diverse as	
SS		
MS		
1,745	stretch beyond	
SS		
MS		
1,746	allows you to	
SS		
MS		

1,747	mitigate the effects of	
SS		
MS		
1,748	a new way to	
SS		
MS		
1,749	how to tackle	
SS		
MS		
1,750	arrive home	
SS		
MS		
1,751	morbidly obese	
SS		
MS		
1,752	can result in	
SS		
MS		

1,753	moderate exercise	
SS		
MS		
1,754	a modicum of	
SS		
MS		
1,755	as loud as	
SS		
MS		
1,756	at the top of	
SS		
MS		
1,757	a hefty dose of	
SS		
MS		
1,758	in addition to	
SS		
MS		

1,759	modulate (one's) voice	
SS		
MS		
1,760	reduce anxiety	
SS		
MS		
1,761	thinking about	
SS		
MS		
1,762	in the beginning stages of	
SS		
MS		
1,763	if left unchecked	
SS		
MS		
1,764	on a regular basis	
SS		
MS		

1,765	not mollified	
SS		
MS		
1,766	driving alone	
SS		
MS		
1,767	through the use of	
SS		
MS		
1,768	an opportunity to	
SS		
MS		
1,769	listening to	
SS		
MS		
1,770	relaxing experience	
SS		
MS		

1,771	daily practice	
SS		
MS		
1,772	it used to be	
SS		
MS		
1,773	needed to	
SS		
MS		
1,774	more enjoyable	
SS		
MS		
1,775	a legal morass	
SS		
MS		
1,776	such a long speech	
SS		
MS		

1,777	multifarious roles	
SS		
MS		
1,778	in such a hurry	
SS		
MS		
1,779	such an admirer of	
SS		
MS		
1,780	showed me the way	
SS		
MS		
1,781	the day before yesterday	
SS		
MS		
1,782	the view from	
SS		
MS		

1,783	mundane matters	
SS		
MS		
1,784	so excited that	
SS		
MS		
1,785	it is no use trying	
SS		
MS		
1,786	it is curious how	
SS		
MS		
1,787	make it a rule to	
SS		
MS		
1,788	the number of mistakes	
SS		
MS		

1,789	the munificence of	
SS		
MS		
1,790	evade the question	
SS		
MS		
1,791	great harm	
SS		
MS		
1,792	tempted to	
SS		
MS		
1,793	a portrait of	
SS		
MS		
1,794	that is no fault of X	
SS		
MS		

1,795	money's worth	
SS		
MS		
1,796	mutable opinions	
SS		
MS		
1,797	a myriad of	
SS		
MS		
1,798	in the mind's eye	
SS		
MS		
1,799	to my heart's content	
SS		
MS		
1,800	from the standpoint of	
SS		
MS		

1,801	the nadir of	
SS		
MS		
1,802	felt out of place	
SS		
MS		
1,803	out of harm's way	
SS		
MS		
1,804	gave six months' notice	
SS		
MS		
1,805	for the happiness of	
SS		
MS		
1,806	the foot of a mountain	
SS		
MS		

1,807	a nascent industry	
SS		
MS		
1,808	the door of the room	
SS		
MS		
1,809	whittle away	
SS		
MS		
1,810	at the botttom of	
SS		
MS		
1,811	in the middle of	
SS		
MS		
1,812	go somewhere	
SS		
MS		

1,813	so nebulous	
SS		
MS		
1,814	blame each other	
SS		
MS		
1,815	make tweaks to	
SS		
MS		
1,816	unaffordable to	
SS		
MS		
1,817	a broad question	
SS		
MS		
1,818	up next is	
SS		
MS		

1,819	nefarious activities	
SS		
MS		
1,820	it's really unbelievable	
SS		
MS		
1,821	the silence was deafening	
SS		
MS		
1,822	obvious threat	
SS		
MS		
1,823	first of all…second of all…	
SS		
MS		
1,824	come out against	
SS		
MS		

1,825	expressed concerns about	
SS		
MS		
1,826	allowed to fester	
SS		
MS		
1,827	a steward of	
SS		
MS		
1,828	ask of (someone)	
SS		
MS		
1,829	knows where the bodies are buried	
SS		
MS		
1,830	lack of preparation	
SS		
MS		

1,831	not particularly sanguine about	
SS		
MS		
1,832	negligent about	
SS		
MS		
1,833	a neophyte when it comes to	
SS		
MS		
1,834	a nocturnal trip	
SS		
MS		
1,835	do tremendous damage	
SS		
MS		
1,836	reasoned that if	
SS		
MS		

1,837	noisome habits	
SS		
MS		
1,838	health hazard	
SS		
MS		
1,839	has absolutely no intention of	
SS		
MS		
1,840	has been at pains to	
SS		
MS		
1,841	an absolute boon for	
SS		
MS		
1,842	no roadmap	
SS		
MS		

1,843	a nomadic tribe	
SS		
MS		
1,844	have a conversation	
SS		
MS		
1,845	was as muh about A as about B	
SS		
MS		
1,846	agreed to produce	
SS		
MS		
1,847	demand obedience	
SS		
MS		
1,848	over the border	
SS		
MS		

1,849	nominal leader	
SS		
MS		
1,850	it is a disaster for	
SS		
MS		
1,851	face popular pressure to	
SS		
MS		
1,852	got back at	
SS		
MS		
1,853	posted a picture	
SS		
MS		
1,854	varying positions	
SS		
MS		

1,855	the nonchalant way in which	
SS		
MS		
1,856	a nondescript office building	
SS		
MS		
1,857	notorious for	
SS		
MS		
1,858	conflicting narratives over	
SS		
MS		
1,859	in thick forest	
SS		
MS		
1,860	in the early hours of	
SS		
MS		

1,861	for a novice	
SS		
MS		
1,862	made it up to	
SS		
MS		
1,863	on Tuesday morning	
SS		
MS		
1,864	effective response	
SS		
MS		
1,865	on the precipice of	
SS		
MS		
1,866	awful numbers	
SS		
MS		

1,867	noxious fumes	
SS		
MS		
1,868	not be surprised if	
SS		
MS		
1,869	on furlough	
SS		
MS		
1,870	does not explain	
SS		
MS		
1,871	a momentary lapse of judgment	
SS		
MS		
1,872	began by telling	
SS		
MS		

1,873	a nuanced commentary	
SS		
MS		
1,874	put heat on	
SS		
MS		
1,875	a long-awaited event	
SS		
MS		
1,876	a long way from	
SS		
MS		
1,877	turned morose	
SS		
MS		
1,878	turned mournful	
SS		
MS		

1,879	nurture children	
SS		
MS		
1,880	an extraordinary afternoon	
SS		
MS		
1,881	in a league of (her) own	
SS		
MS		
1,882	vehemently denied	
SS		
MS		
1,883	a real mistake	
SS		
MS		
1,884	the right priorities	
SS		
MS		

1,885	quite obdurate	
SS		
MS		
1,886	it would be a mistake for	
SS		
MS		
1,887	once seen can't be unseen	
SS		
MS		
1,888	one of the most pivotal figures	
SS		
MS		
1,889	came back for	
SS		
MS		
1,890	gave the full rundown	
SS		
MS		

1,891	obfuscate the issue	
SS		
MS		
1,892	big news	
SS		
MS		
1,893	there's no way	
SS		
MS		
1,894	find time to	
SS		
MS		
1,895	nearing completion	
SS		
MS		
1,896	risk everything to	
SS		
MS		

1,897	an oblique reference to	
SS		
MS		
1,898	so disturbing	
SS		
MS		
1,899	business dealings	
SS		
MS		
1,900	running around in circles	
SS		
MS		
1,901	perfect outlet	
SS		
MS		
1,902	a dumb excuse	
SS		
MS		

1,903	remain oblivious	
SS		
MS		
1,904	obscure books	
SS		
MS		
1,905	an interesting journey	
SS		
MS		
1,906	kudos to	
SS		
MS		
1,907	wasn't all sunshine and rainbows	
SS		
MS		
1,908	day in and day out	
SS		
MS		

1,909	obsequious assistants	
SS		
MS		
1,910	dedicated to	
SS		
MS		
1,911	in the room	
SS		
MS		
1,912	eye witness account	
SS		
MS		
1,913	outdated thinking	
SS		
MS		
1,914	learned a fair amount	
SS		
MS		

1,915	obsolete machinery	
SS		
MS		
1,916	obstinate refusal to	
SS		
MS		
1,917	visibly upset	
SS		
MS		
1,918	an incredible number	
SS		
MS		
1,919	took efforts to pursue	
SS		
MS		
1,920	a long conversation	
SS		
MS		

1,921	obstreperous children	
SS		
MS		
1,922	pushed into	
SS		
MS		
1,923	an orderly way	
SS		
MS		
1,924	act out	
SS		
MS		
1,925	the fact of the matter is	
SS		
MS		
1,926	school boards	
SS		
MS		

1,927	do (one's) best	
SS		
MS		
1,928	too obtuse to	
SS		
MS		
1,929	second to none	
SS		
MS		
1,930	a vital source of	
SS		
MS		
1,931	prone to making	
SS		
MS		
1,932	acted very distraught	
SS		
MS		

1,933	labour under	
SS		
MS		
1,934	odious criminal	
SS		
MS		
1,935	positive impact	
SS		
MS		
1,936	stand silently	
SS		
MS		
1,937	stark differences	
SS		
MS		
1,938	a jigsaw puzzle	
SS		
MS		

1,939	centered around	
SS		
MS		
1,940	an officious assistant	
SS		
MS		
1,941	planned on	
SS		
MS		
1,942	it does seem odd	
SS		
MS		
1,943	less suspicious of	
SS		
MS		
1,944	prompted derision	
SS		
MS		

1,945	ominous clouds	
SS		
MS		
1,946	onerous duty	
SS		
MS		
1,947	it is still possible	
SS		
MS		
1,948	pull out of	
SS		
MS		
1,949	less than	
SS		
MS		
1,950	part of the challenge	
SS		
MS		

1,951	opulent furnishings	
SS		
MS		
1,952	lift up	
SS		
MS		
1,953	found inconsistencies in	
SS		
MS		
1,954	an amazing athlete	
SS		
MS		
1,955	attuned to	
SS		
MS		
1,956	an old view	
SS		
MS		

1,957	delivered an oration	
SS		
MS		
1,958	the notion that	
SS		
MS		
1,959	vowed to challenge	
SS		
MS		
1,960	in the bigger picture	
SS		
MS		
1,961	made a big comeback	
SS		
MS		
1,962	shed no light on	
SS		
MS		

1,963	an ornate writing style	
SS		
MS		
1,964	witness tampering	
SS		
MS		
1,965	for over a decade	
SS		
MS		
1,966	weave a narrtive	
SS		
MS		
1,967	one of two	
SS		
MS		
1,968	under a spotlight	
SS		
S		

1,969	orthodox views on	
SS		
MS		
1,970	laid out	
SS		
MS		
1,971	sensitive language	
SS		
MS		
1,972	stood before	
SS		
MS		
1,973	one big aspect	
SS		
MS		
1,974	throw shade on	
SS		
MS		

1,975	oscillate between A and B	
SS		
MS		
1,976	at the minimum	
SS		
MS		
1,977	a pretty high bar	
SS		
MS		
1,978	remain silent	
SS		
MS		
1,979	seems excessive	
SS		
MS		
1,980	a roadmap for	
SS		
MS		

1,981	the ostensible reason	
SS		
MS		
1,982	ostentatious display	
SS		
MS		
1,983	believe in second chances	
SS		
MS		
1,984	hot button topics	
SS		
MS		
1,985	so fresh	
SS		
MS		
1,986	to the detriment of	
SS		
MS		

1,987	suffered ostracism	
SS		
MS		
1,988	nothing unique about	
SS		
MS		
1,989	bad timing	
SS		
MS		
1,990	disorderly conduct	
SS		
MS		
1,991	line of work	
SS		
MS		
1,992	consenting adults	
SS		
MS		

1,993	ever-before-seen pictures	
SS		
MS		
1,994	antithetical to	
SS		
MS		
1,995	made a poor decision	
SS		
MS		
1,996	reflects poorly on	
SS		
MS		
1,997	forage for	
SS		
MS		
1,998	the greatest impact	
SS		
MS		

1,999	wired for	
SS		
MS		
2,000	a venomous snake	
SS		
MS		
2,001	small wonder that	
SS		
MS		
2,002	a chorus of people	
SS		
MS		
2,003	take the fall for	
SS		
MS		
2,004	doubt every word	
SS		
MS		

2,005	a pacific setting	
SS		
MS		
2,006	really ambitious	
SS		
MS		
2,007	personal reasons	
SS		
MS		
2,008	bad behavior	
SS		
MS		
2,009	sad accident	
SS		
MS		
2,010	all-time favorite	
SS		
MS		

2,011	pacifist beliefs	
SS		
MS		
2,012	especially admire	
SS		
MS		
2,013	hardscrabble life	
SS		
MS		
2,014	very little traction	
SS		
MS		
2,015	just started	
SS		
MS		
2,016	often wonder	
SS		
MS		

2,017	an extraordinary speech	
SS		
MS		
2,018	far less palatable	
SS		
MS		
2,019	a palette for	
SS		
MS		
2,020	warned of	
SS		
MS		
2,021	can palliate	
SS		
MS		
2,022	softly spoken	
SS		
MS		

2,023	a pallid performance	
SS		
MS		
2,024	a panacea for	
SS		
MS		
2,025	a paradigm shift	
SS		
MS		
2,026	seems paradoxical	
SS		
MS		
2,027	quietly spoken	
SS		
MS		
2,028	along with	
SS		
MS		

2,029	walk away	
SS		
MS		
2,030	paragon of virtue	
SS		
MS		
2,031	significant change	
SS		
MS		
2,032	of paramount concern	
SS		
MS		
2,033	unfair advantage	
SS		
MS		
2,034	public attitudes	
SS		
MS		

2,035	a social pariah	
SS		
MS		
2,036	roar back	
SS		
MS		
2,037	unsure how to	
SS		
MS		
2,038	feel uncomfortable	
SS		
MS		
2,039	run out of options	
SS		
MS		
2,040	sidelined by	
SS		
MS		

2,041	a parody of	
SS		
MS		
2,042	the sobering truth	
SS		
MS		
2,043	stand out from the crowd	
SS		
MS		
2,044	looks jarring	
SS		
MS		
2,045	the key to	
SS		
MS		
2,046	complete with	
SS		
MS		

2,047	noticed that	
SS		
MS		
2,048	for most of my childhood	
SS		
MS		
2,049	the parsimony of	
SS		
MS		
2,050	partisan feelings	
SS		
MS		
2,051	freak injury	
SS		
MS		
2,052	causing discomfort	
SS		
MS		

2,053	patent drugs	
SS		
MS		
2,054	the pathology of	
SS		
MS		
2,055	at a conference	
SS		
MS		
2,056	have a way to	
SS		
MS		
2,057	remarked half-jokingly	
SS		
MS		
2,058	won't be fully happy until	
SS		
MS		

2,059	full of pathos	
SS		
MS		
2,060	an ambassador for	
SS		
MS		
2,061	in the future	
SS		
MS		
2,062	patent sincerity	
SS		
MS		
2,063	on command	
SS		
MS		
2,064	transformed by	
SS		
MS		

2,065	paucity of	
SS		
MS		
2,066	genuine curiosity	
SS		
MS		
2,067	a pejorative word	
SS		
MS		
2,068	prove impossible	
SS		
MS		
2,069	wrap around	
SS		
MS		
2,070	doubtful about	
SS		
MS		

2,071	pellucid waters	
SS		
MS		
2,072	a penchant for	
SS		
MS		
2,073	a stroke of good fortune	
SS		
MS		
2,074	up to the task of	
SS		
MS		
2,075	get an early look at	
SS		
MS		
2,076	not longer after	
SS		
MS		

2,077	penitent figure	
SS		
MS		
2,078	hoist myself up	
SS		
MS		
2,079	get the hang of	
SS		
MS		
2,080	one item after another	
SS		
MS		
2,081	there and then	
SS		
MS		
2,082	too much hassle	
SS		
MS		

2,083	penultimate chapter	
SS		
MS		
2,084	a penurious nation	
SS		
MS		
2,085	a profound effect	
SS		
MS		
2,086	a testing time	
SS		
MS		
2,087	weaned off	
SS		
MS		
2,088	pain relief	
SS		
MS		

2,089	a perfidious plot	
SS		
MS		
2,090	a patent falsehood	
SS		
MS		
2,091	over the following days and weeks	
SS		
MS		
2,092	stormed into	
SS		
MS		
2,093	have no recollection of	
SS		
MS		
2,094	vowing not to leave	
SS		
MS		

2,095	a perplexing problem	
SS		
MS		
2,096	a perspicacious counsellor	
SS		
MS		
2,097	flashing lights	
SS		
MS		
2,098	in a matter of hours	
SS		
MS		
2,099	not designed for	
SS		
MS		
2,100	less than a mile away	
SS		
MS		

2,101	a pert retort	
SS		
MS		
2,102	a pertinacious salesperson	
SS		
MS		
2,103	not quite content with	
SS		
MS		
2,104	booked a taxi	
SS		
MS		
2,105	nothing too alarming	
SS		
MS		
2,106	for the first time I can remember	
SS		
MS		

2,107	perusal of	
SS		
MS		
2,108	the sheer pleasure of	
SS		
MS		
2,109	a spring in my step	
SS		
MS		
2,110	put a lot of effort into	
SS		
MS		
2,111	uneven ground	
SS		
MS		
2,112	a ton of questions	
SS		
MS		

2,113	a pervasive odour	
SS		
MS		
2,114	reacted with petulance	
SS		
MS		
2,115	no danger of	
SS		
MS		
2.116	cobbled streets	
SS		
MS		
2,117	fairly simple	
SS		
MS		
2,118	avoid drawing attention	
SS		
MS		

2,119	a philanthropic association	
SS		
MS		
2,120	for most of history	
SS		
MS		
2,121	took delivery of	
SS		
MS		
2,122	nimble fingers	
SS		
MS		
2,123	so clumsy	
SS		
MS		
2,124	more efficient	
SS		
MS		

2,125	phlegmatic personality	
SS		
MS		
2,126	pillaged through	
SS		
MS		
2,127	artificial limbs	
SS		
MS		
2,128	gone through life	
SS		
MS		
2,129	very nearly	
SS		
MS		
2,130	made amazing advances	
SS		
MS		

2,131	pinnacle of	
SS		
MS		
2,132	a pithy saying	
SS		
MS		
2,133	seemed pretty certain that	
SS		
MS		
2,134	a pittance	
SS		
MS		
2,135	a character quirk	
SS		
MS		
2,136	a recipient of	
SS		
MS		

2,137	attempted to placate	
SS		
MS		
2,138	a placid disposition	
SS		
MS		
2,139	need urgent help	
SS		
MS		
2,140	felt compelled to	
SS		
MS		
2,141	those who can't afford	
SS		
MS		
2,142	feeding coins into	
SS		
MS		

2,143	a silly platitude	
SS		
MS		
2,144	flanked by	
SS		
MS		
2,145	a patent falsehood	
SS		
MS		
2,146	in its entirety	
SS		
MS		
2,147	further updates	
SS		
MS		
2,148	crane my neck to	
SS		
MS		

2,149	need to redact	
SS		
MS		
2,150	right way up	
SS		
MS		
2,151	drift through	
SS		
MS		
2,152	received the plaudits of	
SS		
MS		
2,153	licensed to	
SS		
MS		
2,154	reminisced about	
SS		
MS		

2,155	plausible reason	
SS		
MS		
2,156	give orders	
SS		
MS		
2,157	beyond doubt	
SS		
MS		
2,158	denied wrongdoing	
SS		
MS		
2,159	under the influence of	
SS		
MS		
2,160	loop in	
SS		
MS		

2,161	there's a plenitude of	
SS		
MS		
2,162	a plethora of	
SS		
MS		
2,163	shell-shocked by	
SS		
MS		
2,164	pliable parents	
SS		
MS		
2,165	in total shock	
SS		
MS		
2,166	made a prediction about	
SS		
MS		

2,167	a poignant tale	
SS		
MS		
2,168	quite suspenseful	
SS		
MS		
2,169	not convinced that	
SS		
MS		
2,170	continue unimpeded	
SS		
MS		
2,171	a belt and suspenders approach	
SS		
MS		
2,172	duty bound to	
SS		
MS		

2,173	a portent of	
SS		
MS		
2,174	potable water	
SS		
MS		
2,175	publicly release	
SS		
MS		
2,176	news outlet	
SS		
MS		
2,177	showed deference to	
SS		
MS		
2,178	if convicted	
SS		
MS		

2,179	a vulnerable potentate	
SS		
MS		
2,180	the pragmatic attraction	
SS		
MS		
2,181	hobnob with	
SS		
MS		
2,182	once again	
SS		
MS		
2,183	intimidated by	
SS		
MS		
2,184	better informed	
SS		
MS		

2,185	heading to a precipice	
SS		
MS		
2,186	the big enchilada	
SS		
MS		
2,187	in hock to	
SS		
MS		
2,188	connect the dots	
SS		
MS		
2,189	angling for	
SS		
MS		
2,190	a magnet for	
SS		
MS		

2,191	unfit for office	
SS		
MS		
2,192	needn't preclude	
SS		
MS		
2,193	a precocious child	
SS		
MS		
2,194	a predilection for	
SS		
MS		
2,195	poses a real threat	
SS		
MS		
2,196	the week following	
SS		
MS		

2,197	a preponderance of	
SS		
MS		
2,198	prepossessing passion	
SS		
MS		
2,199	doing exactly that	
SS		
MS		
2,200	presaged the arrival of	
SS		
MS		
2,201	spent the night in	
SS		
MS		
2,202	have to pay for	
SS		
MS		

2,203	enough prescient wisdom	
SS		
MS		
2,204	being nice to people	
SS		
MS		
2,205	without words	
SS		
MS		
2,206	a pitcher of water	
SS		
MS		
2,207	dirty deeds	
SS		
MS		
2,208	in the clear	
SS		
MS		

2,209	prescribed medicine	
SS		
MS		
2,210	about to	
SS		
MS		
2,211	comes days before	
SS		
MS		
2,212	a surprise visit	
SS		
MS		
2,213	try to project strength	
SS		
MS		
2,214	not forgiving of	
SS		
MS		

2,215	presumptuous to	
SS		
MS		
2,216	create a ruckus	
SS		
MS		
2,217	the firing of	
SS		
MS		
2,218	the way that	
SS		
MS		
2,219	sit and wait	
SS		
MS		
2,220	can't depend on	
SS		
MS		

2,221	under false pretenses	
SS		
MS		
2,222	likening it to	
SS		
MS		
2,223	more than happy	
SS		
MS		
2,224	known for	
SS		
MS		
2,225	play out	
SS		
MS		
2,226	birds of a feather flock together	
SS		
MS		

2,227	primeval forest	
SS		
MS		
2,228	a life of privation	
SS		
MS		
2,229	very well laid out	
SS		
MS		
2,230	bear false witness against	
SS		
MS		
2,231	a recording device	
SS		
MS		
2,232	on X's behalf	
SS		
MS		

2,233	business probity	
SS		
MS		
2,234	no intention of	
SS		
MS		
2,235	proclivity for	
SS		
MS		
2,236	left the door open to	
SS		
MS		
2,237	cut a deal	
SS		
MS		
2,238	go toe to toe with	
SS		
MS		

2,239	procure information	
SS		
MS		
2,240	met with	
SS		
MS		
2,241	proceed directly to	
SS		
MS		
2,242	fiercely maintain	
SS		
MS		
2,243	impeccable character	
SS		
MS		
2,244	the search for	
SS		
MS		

2,245	a profane rant	
SS		
MS		
2,246	not profligate	
SS		
MS		
2,247	presumption of innocence	
SS		
MS		
2,248	trample upon	
SS		
MS		
2,249	highly qualified	
SS		
MS		
2,250	above all else	
SS		
MS		

2,251	sweated profusely	
SS		
MS		
2,252	have something on	
SS		
MS		
2,253	inflicted damage on	
SS		
MS		
2,254	a sample of	
SS		
MS		
2,255	a stern warning	
SS		
MS		
2,256	there are rumblings that	
SS		
MS		

2,257	promulgated in	
SS		
MS		
2,258	readily propagated	
SS		
MS		
2,259	tamp down expectations	
SS		
MS		
2,260	disapprove of	
SS		
MS		
2,261	don't see why not	
SS		
MS		
2,262	a clean slate	
SS		
MS		

2,263	propensity to	
SS		
MS		
2,264	get reopened	
SS		
MS		
2,265	plenty of	
SS		
MS		
2,266	statute of limitations	
SS		
MS		
2,267	void the agreement	
SS		
MS		
2,268	a clear road map	
SS		
MS		

2,269	a propitious time for	
SS		
MS		
2,270	see a real threat	
SS		
MS		
2,271	fall by the wayside	
SS		
MS		
2,272	a snide remark	
SS		
MS		
2,273	gave more fodder to	
SS		
MS		
2,274	on day one	
SS		
MS		

2,275	the propriety of	
SS		
MS		
2,276	cannot be trusted	
SS		
MS		
2,277	clearly not believable	
SS		
MS		
2,278	have serious doubts about	
SS		
MS		
2,279	couldn't keep (one's) story straight	
SS		
MS		
2,280	make a victory sign	
SS		
MS		

2,281	a prosaic proposal	
SS		
MS		
2,282	proscribed list	
SS		
MS		
2,283	dragged into	
SS		
MS		
2,284	say anything about	
SS		
MS		
2,285	very much agree with	
SS		
MS		
2,286	as obvious as	
SS		
MS		

2,287	starting point	
SS		
MS		
2,288	a protean talent	
SS		
MS		
2,289	quite as helpful	
SS		
MS		
2,290	helpful to	
SS		
MS		
2,291	hardly the case	
SS		
MS		
2,292	public disclosure	
SS		
MS		

2,293	military prowess	
SS		
MS		
2,294	a public perception	
SS		
MS		
2,295	the importance of prudence	
SS		
MS		
2,296	if X is not satisfied	
SS		
MS		
2,297	no there there	
SS		
MS		
2,298	won't commit to making	
SS		
MS		

2,299	prurient interest in	
SS		
MS		
2,300	the rules require	
SS		
MS		
2,301	in eager anticipation	
SS		
MS		
2,302	in preparation for	
SS		
MS		
2,303	no comment	
SS		
MS		
2,304	a wide-ranging interview	
SS		
MS		

2,305	a puerile fantasy	
SS		
MS		
2,306	begins in earnest	
SS		
MS		
2,307	only for pleasure	
SS		
MS		
2,308	take a bit more work	
SS		
MS		
2,309	in human history	
SS		
MS		
2,310	incredibly useful	
SS		
MS		

2,311	buckle up for	
SS		
MS		
2,312	a pugnacious performer	
SS		
MS		
2,313	a glimpse of pulchritude	
SS		
MS		
2,314	punctilious about	
SS		
MS		
2,315	protracted legal battle	
SS		
MS		
2,316	go places	
SS		
MS		

2,317	punitive damages	
SS		
MS		
2,318	connect us to	
SS		
MS		
2,319	the exact opposite	
SS		
MS		
2,320	in that time	
SS		
MS		
2,321	at first annoyed	
SS		
MS		
2,322	the epicenter of	
SS		
MS		

2,323	prey to	
SS		
MS		
2,324	a thousand times	
SS		
MS		
2,325	talk directly to	
SS		
MS		
2,326	less afraid of	
SS		
MS		
2,327	it's such a gift to	
SS		
MS		
2,328	environmental justice	
SS		
MS		

2,329	putrid smell	
SS		
MS		
2,330	hails from	
SS		
MS		
2,331	a much sadder world	
SS		
MS		
2,332	take apart	
SS		
MS		
2,333	one of the greatest pleasures	
SS		
MS		
2,334	at the public library	
SS		
MS		

2,335	sucked into a quagmire	
SS		
MS		
2,336	freely exchange ideas	
SS		
MS		
2,337	how lucky we are	
SS		
MS		
2,338	it's such an extraordinary honour to	
SS		
MS		
2,339	never too old to	
SS		
MS		
2,340	act in the interest of	
SS		
MS		

2,341	a quaint hobby	
SS		
MS		
2,342	in the middle of the street	
SS		
MS		
2,343	written out	
SS		
MS		
2,344	extremely happy	
SS		
MS		
2,345	many times	
SS		
MS		
2,346	happy ending	
SS		
MS		

2,347	in a quandary	
SS		
MS		
2,348	quell anxiety	
SS		
MS		
2,349	carried across	
SS		
MS		
2,350	every branch of knowledge	
SS		
MS		
2,351	making music	
SS		
MS		
2,352	reading out loud	
SS		
MS		

2,353	a querulous person	
SS		
MS		
2,354	a quixotic search for	
SS		
MS		
2,355	so fundamentally important	
SS		
MS		
2,356	guilty by association	
SS		
MS		
2,357	hour of darkness	
SS		
MS		
2,358	tore at	
SS		
MS		

2,359	railed against	
SS		
MS		
2,360	an avid reader	
SS		
MS		
2,361	join the conversation	
SS		
MS		
2,362	(one's) perch at	
SS		
MS		
2,363	a treasure hunt	
SS		
MS		
2,364	bargain books	
SS		
MS		

2,365	rancid butter	
SS		
MS		
2,366	lingering too long	
SS		
MS		
2,367	for the same reason	
SS		
MS		
2,368	had an agreement	
SS		
MS		
2,369	colour outside the lines	
SS		
MS		
2,370	need the assurance of	
SS		
MS		

2,371	without rancor	
SS		
MS		
2,372	build rapport with	
SS		
MS		
2,373	in deep denial	
SS		
MS		
2,374	with skill	
SS		
MS		
2,375	a desire to	
SS		
MS		
2,376	not the center of	
SS		
MS		

2,377	rash decision	
SS		
MS		
2,378	raucous applause	
SS		
MS		
2,379	another way	
SS		
MS		
2,380	stay put	
SS		
MS		
2,381	don't cross	
SS		
MS		
2,382	don't ask	
SS		
MS		

2,383	razed to the ground	
SS		
MS		
2,384	an extraordinary rebuke of	
SS		
MS		
2,385	one of the oddest	
SS		
MS		
2,386	rooting for	
SS		
MS		
2,387	imaginative books	
SS		
MS		
2,388	absolute sincerity	
SS		
MS		

2,389	win leniency	
SS		
MS		
2,390	natural to assume	
SS		
MS		
2,391	convicted in absentia	
SS		
MS		
2,392	perfectly tailored to	
SS		
MS		
2,393	equal access	
SS		
MS		
2,394	a life of reading	
SS		
MS		

2,395	an uncanny ability to	
SS		
MS		
2,396	devoid of	
SS		
MS		
2,397	lose heart	
SS		
MS		
2,398	a straight-up denial	
SS		
MS		
2,399	a flurry of revelations	
SS		
MS		
2,400	act at the behest of	
SS		
MS		

2,401	unfazed by	
SS		
MS		
2,402	a worthy goal	
SS		
MS		
2,403	time of need	
SS		
MS		
2,404	at a crossroads	
SS		
MS		
2,405	intimate details	
SS		
MS		
2,406	hailed as	
SS		
MS		

2,407	the chief concern	
SS		
MS		
2,408	completely innocent	
SS		
MS		
2,409	wild questions	
SS		
MS		
2,410	furious about	
SS		
MS		
2,411	flatly reject	
SS		
MS		
2,412	did an interview	
SS		
MS		

2,413	ambiguous language	
SS		
MS		
2,414	sidestep the question	
SS		
MS		
2,415	incredibly frustrated	
SS		
MS		
2,416	typically includes	
SS		
MS		
2,417	very religious	
SS		
MS		
2,418	dirty cops	
SS		
MS		

2,419	left open the possibility that	
SS		
MS		
2,420	not going to testify	
SS		
MS		
2,421	temporary protection	
SS		
MS		
2,422	extreme positions	
SS		
MS		
2,423	all the more reason why	
SS		
MS		
2,424	wind through	
SS		
MS		

2,425	waged a full-on assault on	
SS		
MS		
2,426	working to regain	
SS		
MS		
2,427	peddling misinformation	
SS		
MS		
2,428	take sole responsibility for	
SS		
MS		
2,429	soft on crime	
SS		
MS		
2,430	tough on crime	
SS		
MS		

2,431	one of my biggest regrets is	
SS		
MS		
2,432	pick up where	
SS		
MS		
2,433	essential government services	
SS		
MS		
2,434	a heated encounter	
SS		
MS		
2,435	passed judgment too quickly	
SS		
MS		
2,436	true nature	
SS		
MS		

2,437	a wandering eye	
SS		
MS		
2,438	had a sit-down with	
SS		
MS		
2,439	a clean set of clothes	
SS		
MS		
2,440	at an impasse	
SS		
MS		
2,441	rejected X out of hand	
SS		
MS		
2,442	the biggest challenge	
SS		
MS		

2,443	diametrically opposed	
SS		
MS		
2,444	at warp speed	
SS		
MS		
2,445	is anybody's guess	
SS		
MS		
2,446	could have a compounding effect	
SS		
MS		
2,447	braced for	
SS		
MS		
2,448	a recalcitrant alcoholic	
SS		
MS		

2,449	ready to reciprocate	
SS		
MS		
2,450	become a thing	
SS		
MS		
2,451	essential to	
SS		
MS		
2,452	a world dominated by	
SS		
MS		
2,453	a flight risk	
SS		
MS		
2,454	warm applause	
SS		
MS		

2,455	a reclusive nation	
SS		
MS		
2,456	reconciled with	
SS		
MS		
2,457	on my travels	
SS		
MS		
2,458	unbeknownst to	
SS		
MS		
2,459	not appropriate	
SS		
MS		
2,460	a pointed question	
SS		
MS		

2,461	an exclusive offer	
SS		
MS		
2,462	did not oppose	
SS		
MS		
2,463	began to erode	
SS		
MS		
2,464	there's a clear sign that	
SS		
MS		
2,465	unshakeable belief	
SS		
MS		
2,466	gain the benefit of	
SS		
MS		

2,467	the path of rectitude	
SS		
MS		
2,468	very quickly	
SS		
MS		
2,469	a profound book	
SS		
MS		
2,470	not sugarcoated	
SS		
MS		
2,471	kindred spirit	
SS		
MS		
2,472	at my desk	
SS		
MS		

2,473	a redoubtable musician	
SS		
MS		
2,474	ideas refracted through	
SS		
MS		
2,475	an improbable beginning	
SS		
MS		
2,476	countless hours	
SS		
MS		
2,477	it is astonishing to	
SS		
MS		
2,478	love of	
SS		
MS		

2,479	refurbished computers	
SS		
MS		
2,480	disdain for	
SS		
MS		
2,481	lost track of	
SS		
MS		
2,482	might be released	
SS		
MS		
2,483	as early as	
SS		
MS		
2,484	at the courthouse	
SS		
MS		

2,485	refute the claims of	
SS		
MS		
2,486	publicly attack	
SS		
MS		
2,487	hanging by a thread	
SS		
MS		
2,488	pled for mercy	
SS		
MS		
2,489	well-known effort	
SS		
MS		
2,490	the final warning	
SS		
MS		

2,491	face expulsion	
SS		
MS		
2,492	close to the finish line	
SS		
MS		
2,493	error strewn	
SS		
MS		
2,494	incredibly competitive	
SS		
MS		
2,495	stare (someone) down	
SS		
MS		
2,496	lay a wreath at	
SS		
MS		

2,497	worth it	
SS		
MS		
2,498	national security	
SS		
MS		
2,499	border wall	
SS		
MS		
2,500	no matter where	
SS		
MS		
2,501	hold the line	
SS		
MS		
2,502	discretionary power	
SS		
MS		

2,503	getting crushed	
SS		
MS		
2,504	a growing sense of dread	
SS		
MS		
2,505	to be fair to	
SS		
MS		
2,506	growing uneasiness	
SS		
MS		
2,507	drag out	
SS		
MS		
2,508	raise the question	
SS		
MS		

2,509	shoulder the burden	
SS		
MS		
2,510	a better negotiator	
SS		
MS		
2,511	higher mark	
SS		
MS		
2,512	an incentive for	
SS		
MS		
2,513	long to	
SS		
MS		
2,514	change everything	
SS		
MS		

2,515	the bottom fell out	
SS		
MS		
2,516	policy disputes	
SS		
MS		
2,517	the former	
SS		
MS		
2,518	the latter	
SS		
MS		
2,519	the right path	
SS		
MS		
2,520	a confidential report	
SS		
MS		

2,521	regurgitated a story about	
SS		
MS		
2,522	relegated to	
SS		
MS		
2,523	provoke anxiety	
SS		
MS		
2,524	sought to determine	
SS		
MS		
2,525	a mercurial person	
SS		
MS		
2,526	one week from now	
SS		
MS		

2,527	relish travelling	
SS		
MS		
2,528	remedial classes	
SS		
MS		
2,529	a very good week for	
SS		
MS		
2,530	no matter how you slice it	
SS		
MS		
2,531	minimum wage	
SS		
MS		
2,532	under arrest	
SS		
MS		

2,533	it would be remiss of me	
SS		
MS		
2,534	rule the night	
SS		
MS		
2,535	a newly renovated	
SS		
MS		
2,536	moving around	
SS		
MS		
2,537	sprawling town	
SS		
MS		
2,538	conflicting information	
SS		
MS		

2,539	of great renown	
SS		
MS		
2,540	renunciation of	
SS		
MS		
2,541	in that moment	
SS		
MS		
2,542	tinted windows	
SS		
MS		
2,543	the true meaning of	
SS		
MS		
2,544	go to ground	
SS		
MS		

2,545	seemed genuinely repentant	
SS		
MS		
2,546	slipped through the fingers	
SS		
MS		
2,547	close to	
SS		
MS		
2,548	make informed decisions	
SS		
MS		
2,549	in place	
SS		
MS		
2,550	on the brink of	
SS		
MS		

2,551	replete with	
SS		
MS		
2,552	had a vague idea of	
SS		
MS		
2,553	it is remarkable that	
SS		
MS		
2,554	deeply obscure	
SS		
MS		
2,555	stood by silently	
SS		
MS		
2,556	so disrespectful	
SS		
MS		

2,557	in perfect repose	
SS		
MS		
2,558	reprehensible acts	
SS		
MS		
2,559	a tradition of hospitality	
SS		
MS		
2,560	very unhappy that	
SS		
MS		
2,561	skirt the rules	
SS		
MS		
2,562	brought to light	
SS		
MS		

2,563	under no obligation to	
SS		
MS		
2,564	got a reprieve	
SS		
MS		
2,565	run out the clock	
SS		
MS		
2,566	beyond reproach	
SS		
MS		
2,567	a reprobate lifestyle	
SS		
MS		
2,568	don't give ground on	
SS		
MS		

2,569	a reproving look	
SS		
MS		
2,570	repudiated the allegations	
SS		
MS		
2,571	the initial response	
SS		
MS		
2,572	must be true	
SS		
MS		
2,573	not a fan of	
SS		
MS		
2,574	wait and wonder	
SS		
MS		

2,575	on several occasions	
SS		
MS		
2,576	made several errors	
SS		
MS		
2,577	repulsed by	
SS		
MS		
2,578	a reputable brand	
SS		
MS		
2,579	made a requisition for	
SS		
MS		
2,580	scored a huge victory	
SS		
MS		

2,581	come clean	
SS		
MS		
2,582	have very little recourse	
SS		
MS		
2,583	rescind the offer	
SS		
MS		
2,584	reservoir of	
SS		
MS		
2,585	boggles the mind	
SS		
MS		
2,586	my best guess	
SS		
MS		

2,587	more resilient	
SS		
MS		
2,588	search warrant	
SS		
MS		
2,589	quiet but resolute	
SS		
MS		
2,590	a character flaw	
SS		
MS		
2,591	grudge against	
SS		
MS		
2,592	personal grievance	
SS		
MS		

2,593	keep talking about	
SS		
MS		
2,594	resolved to	
SS		
MS		
2,595	enthusiastic response	
SS		
MS		
2,596	respite from	
SS		
MS		
2,597	across the board	
SS		
MS		
2,598	proud to have	
SS		
MS		

2,599	resplendent in	
SS		
MS		
2,600	sought restitution for	
SS		
MS		
2,601	an unfortunate outcome	
SS		
MS		
2,602	not really a big deal	
SS		
MS		
2,603	gain on	
SS		
MS		
2,604	a big surprise	
SS		
MS		

2,605	wilful blindness	
SS		
MS		
2,606	the family breadwinner	
SS		
MS		
2,607	failed to retract	
SS		
MS		
2,608	revel in	
SS		
MS		
2,609	have a lot of time on (one's) hands	
SS		
MS		
2,610	have serious doubts	
SS		
MS		

2,611	sleeping partner	
SS		
MS		
2,612	yearn for	
SS		
MS		
2,613	a battle of wills	
SS		
MS		
2,614	not least	
SS		
MS		
2,615	revered as	
SS		
MS		
2,616	for no good reason	
SS		
MS		

2,617	threatened to revoke	
SS		
MS		
2,618	rhapsodized about	
SS		
MS		
2,619	highly amusing	
SS		
MS		
2,620	turned heads	
SS		
MS		
2,621	never admitted X to	
SS		
MS		
2,622	beggar belief	
SS		
MS		

2,623	rule out	
SS		
MS		
2,624	ribald jokes	
SS		
MS		
2,625	adhere loosely	
SS		
MS		
2,626	rife with	
SS		
MS		
2,627	spring up	
SS		
MS		
2,628	on the subject of	
SS		
MS		

2,629	ruminated over	
SS		
MS		
2,630	a blessed relief	
SS		
MS		
2,631	a clever ruse	
SS		
MS		
2,632	a saccharine smile	
SS		
MS		
2,633	a sacrosanct institution	
SS		
MS		
2,634	purporting to be	
SS		
MS		

2,635	the sagacity of	
SS		
MS		
2,636	widespread use of	
SS		
MS		
2,637	the salient facts	
SS		
MS		
2,638	took hold	
SS		
MS		
2,639	a common salutation	
SS		
MS		
2,640	generally speaking	
SS		
MS		

2,641	salved the pain	
SS		
MS		
2,642	the nuts and bolts	
SS		
MS		
2,643	prevalent in	
SS		
MS		
2,644	wait patiently	
SS		
MS		
2,645	an awfully long time	
SS		
MS		
2,646	devised to	
SS		
MS		

2,647	a sanctimonious lecture	
SS		
MS		
2,648	sanguine about	
SS		
MS		
2,649	a bit sloppy	
SS		
MS		
2,650	can be conflated into	
SS		
MS		
2,651	very modish	
SS		
MS		
2,652	the fount of	
SS		
MS		

2,653	to a greater degree	
SS		
MS		
2,654	misconceptions about	
SS		
MS		
2,655	never satiated	
SS		
MS		
2,656	open the door	
SS		
MS		
2,657	a scathing comment	
SS		
MS		
2,658	false hope	
SS		
MS		

2,659	amount to	
SS		
MS		
2,660	a scintillating discussion	
SS		
MS		
2,661	a key exception	
SS		
MS		
2,662	scurrilous rumors	
SS		
MS		
2,663	a grave problem	
SS		
MS		
2,664	hunt down	
SS		
MS		

2,665	entry point	
SS		
MS		
2,666	a sedentary lifestyle	
SS		
MS		
2,667	fishing for compliments	
SS		
MS		
2,668	unlikely to happen	
SS		
MS		
2,669	a seminal book	
SS		
MS		
2,670	dig around	
SS		
MS		

2,671	sensual desires	
SS		
MS		
2,672	serendipity involved in	
SS		
MS		
2,673	serene skies	
SS		
MS		
2,674	can't bear	
SS		
MS		
2,675	log off from	
SS		
MS		
2,676	a curious case	
SS		
MS		

2,677	servile attitude	
SS		
MS		
2,678	a sinuous road	
SS		
MS		
2,679	a sobriety tet	
SS		
MS		
2,680	a look back through	
SS		
MS		
2,681	sheer luck	
SS		
MS		
2,682	tried to solve	
SS		
MS		

2,683	try to understand	
SS		
MS		
2,684	solicitous inquiry	
SS		
MS		
2,685	a game of chance	
SS		
MS		
2,686	an incredibly significant	
SS		
MS		
2,687	err on the side of	
SS		
MS		
2,688	a solipsistic view	
SS		
MS		

2,689	defective heart	
SS		
MS		
2,690	spend time	
SS		
MS		
2,691	a soluble problem	
SS		
MS		
2,692	couldn't see	
SS		
MS		
2,693	not really sure if	
SS		
MS		
2,694	legal hurdles	
SS		
MS		

2,695	potential for confusion	
SS		
MS		
2,696	stay solvent	
SS		
MS		
2,697	an absolute nightmare	
SS		
MS		
2,698	a somnolent speech	
SS		
MS		
2,699	a sophomoric joke	
SS		
MS		
2,700	so much so	
SS		
MS		

2,701	a sovereign state	
SS		
MS		
2,702	an incredible challenge	
SS		
MS		
2,703	purely speculative	
SS		
MS		
2,704	pretty similar	
SS		
MS		
2,705	wasn't the same for	
SS		
MS		
2,706	spurious claims	
SS		
MS		

2,707	of middling popularity	
SS		
MS		
2,708	in the tank	
SS		
MS		
2,709	solid numbers	
SS		
MS		
2,710	show an inclination to	
SS		
MS		
2,711	show an inclination for	
SS		
MS		
2,712	partially closed	
SS		
MS		

2,713	absolutely no problem	
SS		
MS		
2,714	political spectacle	
SS		
MS		
2,715	have the spine to	
SS		
MS		
2,716	public opinion	
SS		
MS		
2,717	an open secret	
SS		
MS		
2,718	business as usual	
SS		
MS		

2,719	a test of wills	
SS		
MS		
2,720	a new generation	
SS		
MS		
2,721	feel forgotten	
SS		
MS		
2,722	rocket to the top	
SS		
MS		
2,723	a particular message	
SS		
MS		
2,724	an outstanding person	
SS		
MS		

2,725	electrified by	
SS		
MS		
2,726	more invigorated	
SS		
MS		
2,727	will not take place	
SS		
MS		
2,728	in the coming hours	
SS		
MS		
2,729	furloughed workers	
SS		
MS		
2,730	a pipeline of	
SS		
MS		

2,731	by talking to	
SS		
MS		
2,732	evidence of	
SS		
MS		
2,733	dozens of people	
SS		
MS		
2,734	peel away from	
SS		
MS		
2,735	sneak into	
SS		
MS		
2,736	tremendous experience	
SS		
MS		

2,737	well-cared for	
SS		
MS		
2,738	expressed despair over	
SS		
MS		
2,739	for deterrence purposes	
SS		
MS		
2,740	lasting trauma	
SS		
MS		
2,741	chief of staff	
SS		
MS		
2,742	a fishing expedition	
SS		
MS		

2,743	not interfere with	
SS		
MS		
2,744	pose a threat to	
SS		
MS		
2,745	a disgraceful performance	
SS		
MS		
2,746	within reason	
SS		
MS		
2,747	funnel information to	
SS		
MS		
2,748	it strains credibility that	
SS		
MS		

2,749	legal jeopardy	
SS		
MS		
2,750	official capacity	
SS		
MS		
2,751	stagnating water	
SS		
MS		
2,752	one of the things that is a challenge	
SS		
MS		
2,753	staid demeanour	
SS		
MS		
2,754	a crucial part	
SS		
MS		

2,755	too stingy	
SS		
MS		
2,756	blown away by	
SS		
MS		
2,757	a bit of relaxation	
SS		
MS		
2,758	collect information	
SS		
MS		
2,759	went on several journeys	
SS		
MS		
2,760	a forgotten figure	
SS		
MS		

2,761	explained how	
SS		
MS		
2,762	fish market	
SS		
MS		
2,763	new way of thinking	
SS		
MS		
2,764	a stoic expression	
SS		
MS		
2,765	dusted off	
SS		
MS		
2,766	slipped through the cracks	
SS		
MS		

2,767	has good intentions	
SS		
MS		
2,768	in possession of	
SS		
MS		
2,769	rarely seen	
SS		
MS		
2,770	in an effort to undermine	
SS		
MS		
2,771	tipped the scales at	
SS		
MS		
2,772	experience the stigma of	
SS		
MS		

2,773	call it quits	
SS		
MS		
2,774	contract extension	
SS		
MS		
2,775	trade barbs with	
SS		
MS		
2,776	classified as	
SS		
MS		
2,777	a thorough investigation	
SS		
MS		
2,778	require A and B in equal measure	
SS		
MS		

2,779	remained stolid during	
SS		
MS		
2,780	much-talked about	
SS		
MS		
2,781	baffled by	
SS		
MS		
2,782	distaste for	
SS		
MS		
2,783	strenuous exercise	
SS		
MS		
2,784	rose to prominence	
SS		
MS		

2,785	strident voice	
SS		
MS		
2,786	alleged attack	
SS		
MS		
2,787	square the circle	
SS		
MS		
2,788	very satisfied	
SS		
MS		
2,789	took a dig at	
SS		
MS		
2,790	take potshots at	
SS		
MS		

2,791	extraordinarily conscientious	
SS		
MS		
2,792	a wide variety of	
SS		
MS		
2,793	a surprising attack on	
SS		
MS		
2,794	push past	
SS		
MS		
2,795	for the time being	
SS		
MS		
2,796	stupefied expression	
SS		
MS		

2,797	stiff competition	
SS		
MS		
2,798	a system that subjugates	
SS		
MS		
2,799	fold in half	
SS		
MS		
2,800	an important milestone	
SS		
MS		
2,801	sublime beauty	
SS		
MS		
2,802	voice concern over	
SS		
MS		

2,803	will not be allowed	
SS		
MS		
2,804	a submissive person	
SS		
MS		
2,805	take meaningful steps to	
SS		
MS		
2,806	a succinct description	
SS		
MS		
2,807	fairly consistently	
SS		
MS		
2,808	see how far (one) can go	
SS		
MS		

2,809	go for broke	
SS		
MS		
2,810	striving for	
SS		
MS		
2,811	a superfluous detail	
SS		
MS		
2,812	a decent person	
SS		
MS		
2,813	a surfeit of	
SS		
MS		
2,814	a pleasant life	
SS		
MS		

2,815	a compelling essay	
SS		
MS		
2,816	surmised that	
SS		
MS		
2,817	a furious reaction	
SS		
MS		
2,818	get suspicious about	
SS		
MS		
2,819	surreptitious meeting	
SS		
MS		
2,820	ethical lapse	
SS		
MS		

2,821	under a microscope	
SS		
MS		
2,822	there was no way	
SS		
MS		
2,823	surrogate mother	
SS		
MS		
2,824	accountable for	
SS		
MS		
2,825	swarthy complexion	
SS		
MS		
2,826	at the head of	
SS		
MS		

2,827	on what grounds	
SS		
MS		
2,828	the whole gamut	
SS		
MS		
2,829	providing evidence	
SS		
MS		
2,830	sycophantic praise	
SS		
MS		
2,831	make important decisions	
SS		
MS		
2,832	answer for	
SS		
MS		

2,833	will happen at	
SS		
MS		
2,834	tacit agreement	
SS		
MS		
2,835	genius move	
SS		
MS		
2,836	a taciturn child	
SS		
MS		
2,837	live out loud	
SS		
MS		
2,838	a tangential point	
SS		
MS		

2,839	looming over	
SS		
MS		
2,840	tantamount to	
SS		
MS		
2,841	public figure	
SS		
MS		
2,842	until this moment	
SS		
MS		
2,843	top-notch medical care	
SS		
MS		
2,844	endured negative scrutiny	
SS		
MS		

2,845	put (something) on hold	
SS		
MS		
2,846	never stopped	
SS		
MS		
2,847	expansive grounds	
SS		
MS		
2,848	there's no doubt	
SS		
MS		
2,849	give ground	
SS		
MS		
2,850	worked crazy hours	
SS		
MS		

2,851	wear (one's) heart on one's sleeves	
SS		
MS		
2,852	a tedious speech	
SS		
MS		
2,853	have the temerity to	
SS		
MS		
2,854	pretty sore	
SS		
MS		
2,855	culture of respect	
SS		
MS		
2,856	put others first	
SS		
MS		

2,857	a happy childhood	
SS		
MS		
2,858	marked by temperance	
SS		
MS		
2,859	filled with dread	
SS		
MS		
2,860	a healing balm	
SS		
MS		
2,861	no longer tenable	
SS		
MS		
2,862	hasn't changed	
SS		
MS		

2,863	isn't pleasant	
SS		
MS		
2,864	a tenuous relationship	
SS		
MS		
2,865	terrestrial birds	
SS		
MS		
2,866	more restrained	
SS		
MS		
2,867	a timorous voice	
SS		
MS		
2,868	a bit over-effusive	
SS		
MS		

2,869	a bit tiresome	
SS		
MS		
2,870	directed a tirade at	
SS		
MS		
2,871	a great gift	
SS		
MS		
2,872	have sleepless nights	
SS		
MS		
2,873	a real toady	
SS		
MS		
2,874	get nervous	
SS		
MS		

2,875	a major tome on	
SS		
MS		
2,876	unspecified role	
SS		
MS		
2,877	torrid weather	
SS		
MS		
2,878	a tortuous path	
SS		
MS		
2,879	over recent years	
SS		
MS		
2,880	run of the mill	
SS		
MS		

2,881	call it quits	
SS		
MS		
2,882	plagued by fear	
SS		
MS		
2,883	feigned delight	
SS		
MS		
2,884	dusk was starting to fall	
SS		
MS		
2,885	you and I	
SS		
MS		
2,886	closest friend	
SS		
MS		

2,887	a humane policy	
SS		
MS		
2,888	outrageous levels of	
SS		
MS		
2,889	a tractable horse	
SS		
MS		
2,890	energy efficiency	
SS		
MS		
2,891	an intractable infection	
SS		
MS		
2,892	existential threat	
SS		
MS		

2,893	need leadership	
SS		
MS		
2,894	extended family	
SS		
MS		
2,895	a huge influence	
SS		
MS		
2,896	tranquil lake	
SS		
MS		
2,897	progressive tax system	
SS		
MS		
2,898	regressive tax system	
SS		
MS		

2,899	cramped apartment	
SS		
MS		
2,900	extremely cheap	
SS		
MS		
2,901	reveal details about	
SS		
MS		
2,902	sweep to power	
SS		
MS		
2,903	a transient population	
SS		
MS		
2,904	a dedicated following	
SS		
MS		

2,905	get through	
SS		
MS		
2,906	not fun and games	
SS		
MS		
2,907	transmuted into	
SS		
MS		
2,908	respond thoughtfully	
SS		
MS		
2,909	travesty of justice	
SS		
MS		
2,910	tried mightily to	
SS		
MS		

2,911	paid to	
SS		
MS		
2,912	walk off the job	
SS		
MS		
2,913	increased risk of	
SS		
MS		
2,914	screen time	
SS		
MS		
2,915	under the age of	
SS		
MS		
2,916	gust of wind	
SS		
MS		

2,917	tremulous hands	
SS		
MS		
2,918	trenchant analysis	
SS		
MS		
2,919	change of leadership	
SS		
MS		
2,920	makes it hard to	
SS		
MS		
2,921	the root cause	
SS		
MS		
2,922	in need	
SS		
MS		

2,923	off the grid	
SS		
MS		
2,924	a limited number	
SS		
MS		
2,925	easier to afford	
SS		
MS		
2,926	on average	
SS		
MS		
2,927	get hooked	
SS		
MS		
2,928	with trepidation	
SS		
MS		

2,929	continue to try	
SS		
MS		
2,930	abject surrender	
SS		
MS		
2,931	far from trite	
SS		
MS		
2,932	keep (one's) fingers on the pulse of	
SS		
MS		
2,933	get crosswise with	
SS		
MS		
2,934	have expectations about	
SS		
MS		

2,935	take solace in the fact that	
SS		
MS		
2,936	good relationships	
SS		
MS		
2,937	clutch (one's) pearls	
SS		
MS		
2,938	an innocent person	
SS		
MS		
2,939	pay for	
SS		
MS		
2,940	get summoned	
SS		
MS		

2,941	a textbook operation	
SS		
MS		
2,942	in the soup	
SS		
MS		
2,943	a segment of	
SS		
MS		
2,944	political realm	
SS		
MS		
2,945	is in question	
SS		
MS		
2,946	a truncated discussion	
SS		
MS		

2,947	defy (someone) openly	
SS		
MS		
2,948	to put it mildly	
SS		
MS		
2,949	under enormous pressure	
SS		
MS		
2,950	cozy up to	
SS		
MS		
2,951	seem indispensable	
SS		
MS		
2,952	hold up	
SS		
MS		

2,953	hardcore supporter	
SS		
MS		
2,954	for want of a better word	
SS		
MS		
2,955	the best option	
SS		
MS		
2,956	wind up with	
SS		
MS		
2,957	autonomous vehicles	
SS		
MS		
2,958	think ahead	
SS		
MS		

2,959	forgo travel	
SS		
MS		
2,960	in the gloom	
SS		
MS		
2,961	turgid limbs	
SS		
MS		
2,962	withering criticism	
SS		
MS		
2,963	stay behind	
SS		
MS		
2,964	a bizarre performance	
SS		
MS		

2,965	acts of turpitude	
SS		
MS		
2,966	denied knowing	
SS		
MS		
2,967	a great decision	
SS		
MS		
2,968	every aspect	
SS		
MS		
2,969	lobbying for	
SS		
MS		
2,970	really tough	
SS		
MS		

2,971	the overwhelming majority	
SS		
MS		
2,972	wield power	
SS		
MS		
2,973	without a hint of	
SS		
MS		
2,974	direct contact	
SS		
MS		
2,975	went far beyond	
SS		
MS		
2,976	reunited with	
SS		
MS		

2,977	as the meeting began	
SS		
MS		
2,978	relay a message	
SS		
MS		
2,979	on the job	
SS		
MS		
2,980	emergency declaration	
SS		
MS		
2,981	undivided support	
SS		
MS		
2,982	the latest news	
SS		
MS		

2,983	a side street	
SS		
MS		
2,984	time and time again	
SS		
MS		
2,985	too awful	
SS		
MS		
2,986	time immemorial	
SS		
MS		
2,987	ubiquitous computing	
SS		
MS		
2,988	doomed to	
SS		
MS		

2,989	as firm as	
SS		
MS		
2,990	take umbrage at	
SS		
MS		
2,991	resort to	
SS		
MS		
2,992	unctuous salesman	
SS		
MS		
2,993	undulating hills	
SS		
MS		
2,994	excited customers	
SS		
MS		

2,995	thronged with	
SS		
MS		
2,996	the necessity of	
SS		
MS		
2,997	inattention to	
SS		
MS		
2,998	unlucky alliance	
SS		
MS		
2,999	head back	
SS		
MS		
3,000	scout out	
SS		
MS		

3,001	greedy for	
SS		
MS		
3,002	a different sort of	
SS		
MS		
3,003	in store for	
SS		
MS		
3,004	foreign territory	
SS		
MS		
3,005	all at once	
SS		
MS		
3,006	the howl of	
SS		
MS		

3,007	dreamed of	
SS		
MS		
3,008	upbraided by	
SS		
MS		
3,009	piled up	
SS		
MS		
3,010	unfathomable to	
SS		
MS		
3,011	out-of-pocket expenses	
SS		
MS		
3,012	in vain	
SS		
MS		

3,013	absolutely convinced	
SS		
MS		
3,014	volunteered for	
SS		
MS		
3,015	talk about	
SS		
MS		
3,016	a late-night call	
SS		
MS		
3,017	lost consciousness	
SS		
MS		
3,018	came out	
SS		
MS		

3,019	crowd out	
SS		
MS		
3,020	during the winter	
SS		
MS		
3,021	began with	
SS		
MS		
3,022	think in terms of	
SS		
MS		
3,023	difficult to reach	
SS		
MS		
3,024	not up to	
SS		
MS		

3,025	along the way	
SS		
MS		
3,026	thrown overboard	
SS		
MS		
3,027	often told	
SS		
MS		
3,028	not uncommon for	
SS		
MS		
3,029	everyday life	
SS		
MS		
3,030	strewn about	
SS		
MS		

3,031	as it is	
SS		
MS		
3,032	an intolerable point	
SS		
MS		
3,033	the cornerstone of	
SS		
MS		
3,034	bit by bit	
SS		
MS		
3,035	on the coattails of	
SS		
MS		
3,036	bid farewell to	
SS		
MS		

3,037	erected to	
SS		
MS		
3,038	belong to	
SS		
MS		
3,039	in the end	
SS		
MS		
3,040	renewal of	
SS		
MS		
3,041	keep a watchful eye	
SS		
MS		
3,042	more often than not	
SS		
MS		

3,043	couldn't have	
SS		
MS		
3,044	inoculated against	
SS		
MS		
3,045	attempted to usurp	
SS		
MS		
3,046	without a trace	
SS		
MS		
3,047	more than once	
SS		
MS		
3,048	can't say that	
SS		
MS		

3,049	no incentive for	
SS		
MS		
3,050	utilitarian furniture	
SS		
MS		
3,051	out of the blue	
SS		
MS		
3,052	until the end	
SS		
MS		
3,053	argued with	
SS		
MS		
3,054	a few weeks	
SS		
MS		

3,055	incompatible with	
SS		
MS		
3,056	vacillate between A and B	
SS		
MS		
3,057	lived near	
SS		
MS		
3,058	nothing but	
SS		
MS		
3,059	badly burned	
SS		
MS		
3,060	so upset	
SS		
MS		

3,061	continued to	
SS		
MS		
3,062	had a falling out	
SS		
MS		
3,063	a world of	
SS		
MS		
3,064	none of	
SS		
MS		
3,065	jejune performance	
SS		
MS		
3,066	come evening	
SS		
MS		

3,067	since childhood	
SS		
MS		
3,068	validated by	
SS		
MS		
3,069	stand alone	
SS		
MS		
3,070	change gears	
SS		
MS		
3,071	public remarks	
SS		
MS		
3,072	a gag order	
SS		
MS		

3,073	drop the hammer on	
SS		
MS		
3,074	erased any doubt about	
SS		
MS		
3,075	do a tremendous job	
SS		
MS		
3,076	a bizarre moment	
SS		
MS		
3,077	get a fair shake	
SS		
MS		
3,078	didn't need to	
SS		
MS		

3,079	tamper with	
SS		
MS		
3,080	vapid lyrics	
SS		
MS		
3,081	compounded by	
SS		
MS		
3,082	crushing defeat	
SS		
MS		
3,083	a national emergency	
SS		
MS		
3,084	desperately hoped	
SS		
MS		

3,085	should be spent on	
SS		
MS		
3,086	a building project	
SS		
MS		
3,087	variegated leaves	
SS		
MS		
3,088	pretty easy to	
SS		
MS		
3,089	not getting	
SS		
MS		
3,090	as clear as	
SS		
MS		

3,091	took to Twitter	
SS		
MS		
3,092	protested vehemently	
SS		
MS		
3,093	a possible threat to	
SS		
MS		
3,094	few parallels	
SS		
MS		
3,095	an ardent defender	
SS		
MS		
3,096	a striking scene	
SS		
MS		

3,097	stress relief	
SS		
MS		
3,098	verbal attacks	
SS		
MS		
3,099	at one time	
SS		
MS		
3,100	needs therapy	
SS		
MS		
3,101	a sad moment	
SS		
MS		
3,102	unique to	
SS		
MS		

3,103	unusually high number of	
SS		
MS		
3,104	presumed to be	
SS		
MS		
3,105	veneer of sophistication	
SS		
MS		
3,106	prescription drugs	
SS		
MS		
3,107	speak openly about	
SS		
MS		
3,108	without precedence	
SS		
MS		

3,109	more available	
SS		
MS		
3,110	pain and anguish	
SS		
MS		
3,111	felt threatened	
SS		
MS		
3,112	the huge popularity of	
SS		
MS		
3,113	amassed from	
SS		
MS		
3,114	mental health	
SS		
MS		

3,115	social angst	
SS		
MS		
3,116	often blamed for	
SS		
MS		
3,117	an intermediary	
SS		
MS		
3,118	a venerable tradition	
SS		
MS		
3,119	follow leads	
SS		
MS		
3,120	wait a few days	
SS		
MS		

3,121	of one mind	
SS		
MS		
3,122	the veracity of	
SS		
MS		
3,123	a verbose speaker	
SS		
MS		
3,124	backed by	
SS		
MS		
3,125	any further attack	
SS		
MS		
3,126	praised as	
SS		
MS		

3,127	obtain a better picture of	
SS		
MS		
3,128	not known to	
SS		
MS		
3,129	an active police investigation	
SS		
MS		
3,130	brought to the attention of	
SS		
MS		
3,131	important questions	
SS		
MS		
3,132	in hindsight	
SS		
MS		

3,133	high vigilance	
SS		
MS		
3,134	in support	
SS		
MS		
3,135	in comfort	
SS		
MS		
3,136	verdant campus	
SS		
MS		
3,137	crossed X on	
SS		
MS		
3,138	a horrendous event	
SS		
MS		

3,139	a vexing problem	
SS		
MS		
3,140	certain that	
SS		
MS		
3,141	a victim of	
SS		
MS		
3,142	made a decision about	
SS		
MS		
3,143	incredibly proud	
SS		
MS		
3,144	a barrage of tears	
SS		
MS		

3,145	get attention	
SS		
MS		
3,146	a near-miss	
SS		
MS		
3,147	a quick fix	
SS		
MS		
3,148	raise hope	
SS		
MS		
3,149	fall far short of	
SS		
MS		
3,150	disputed by	
SS		
MS		

3,151	did not consent to	
SS		
MS		
3,152	call for action	
SS		
MS		
3,153	a one-time payment	
SS		
MS		
3,154	after years of inaction	
SS		
MS		
3,155	a rude bore	
SS		
MS		
3,156	a polite person	
SS		
MS		

3,157	became teetotal	
SS		
MS		
3,158	great depth of anguish	
SS		
MS		
3,159	beginning to accept	
SS		
MS		
3,160	even larger than	
SS		
MS		
3,161	absolutely decimated	
SS		
MS		
3,162	a significant part of	
SS		
MS		

3,163	practically everything	
SS		
MS		
3,164	in as many months	
SS		
MS		
3,165	the affected areas	
SS		
MS		
3,166	declared a state of emergency	
SS		
MS		
3,167	quite frustrated	
SS		
MS		
3,168	was hoping	
SS		
MS		

3,169	consigned to	
SS		
MS		
3,170	notified that	
SS		
MS		
3,171	provided satisfactory relief to	
SS		
MS		
3,172	just how fickle	
SS		
MS		
3,173	learning about	
SS		
MS		
3,174	a criminal probe	
SS		
MS		

3,175	a portion of	
SS		
MS		
3,176	very careful in	
SS		
MS		
3,177	has a duty to	
SS		
MS		
3,178	more details about	
SS		
MS		
3,179	several sources say	
SS		
MS		
3,180	cannot comment on	
SS		
MS		

3,181	came on the heels of	
SS		
MS		
3,182	from the night before	
SS		
MS		
3,183	several years ago	
SS		
MS		
3,184	helped rescue	
SS		
MS		
3,185	submerged under	
SS		
MS		
3,186	completely engulfed	
SS		
MS		

3,187	unaccounted for	
SS		
MS		
3,188	the most affected area	
SS		
MS		
3,189	before moving to	
SS		
MS		
3,190	without further explanation	
SS		
MS		
3,191	ordered by a judge to	
SS		
MS		
3,192	risen to	
SS		
MS		

3,193	ferocious winds	
SS		
MS		
3,194	many more	
SS		
MS		
3,195	in a rare interview	
SS		
MS		
3,196	voiced concerns about	
SS		
MS		
3,197	became increasingly anxious	
SS		
MS		
3,198	a thinly-veiled ultimatum	
SS		
MS		

3,199	pressure X to	
SS		
MS		
3,200	constant risk	
SS		
MS		
3,201	increasingly centered around	
SS		
MS		
3,202	growing influence	
SS		
MS		
3,203	concerns about	
SS		
MS		
3,204	through fear and coercion	
SS		
MS		

3,205	a prominent event	
SS		
MS		
3,206	lined up to	
SS		
MS		
3,207	has absolutely no interest in	
SS		
MS		
3,208	hand over	
SS		
MS		
3,209	bluntly accused X of	
SS		
MS		
3,210	cannot afford to	
SS		
MS		

3,211	unlikely to	
SS		
MS		
3,212	worst day	
SS		
MS		
3,213	freak (someone) out	
SS		
MS		
3,214	an insecure person	
SS		
MS		
3,215	no such thing as	
SS		
MS		
3,216	caught by surprise	
SS		
MS		

3,217	obtained by	
SS		
MS		
3,218	charged with	
SS		
MS		
3,219	looks a lot like	
SS		
MS		
3,220	take it down a notch	
SS		
MS		
3,221	left open the possibility of	
SS		
MS		
3,222	the exception	
SS		
MS		

3,223	seemed to be	
SS		
MS		
3,224	put under a microscope	
SS		
MS		
3,225	different from	
SS		
MS		
3,226	the prospect of	
SS		
MS		
3,227	turned down	
SS		
MS		
3,228	intended to	
SS		
MS		

3,229	closer to home	
SS		
MS		
3,230	just before	
SS		
MS		
3,231	across the globe	
SS		
MS		
3,232	surprising victory	
SS		
MS		
3,233	hail from	
SS		
MS		
3,234	brush off	
SS		
MS		

3,235	work their way through	
SS		
MS		
3,236	cause headache for	
SS		
MS		
3,237	surpassed expectations	
SS		
MS		
3,238	still underway	
SS		
MS		
3,239	put a damper on	
SS		
MS		
3,240	come at a time when	
SS		
MS		

3,241	a review of	
SS		
MS		
3,242	undocumented workers	
SS		
MS		
3,243	attracted protests	
SS		
MS		
3,244	removed from	
SS		
MS		
3,245	nearly imperceptible	
SS		
MS		
3,246	pleaded guilty to	
SS		
MS		

3,247	under scrutiny from	
SS		
MS		
3,248	character witnesses	
SS		
MS		
3,249	pry off	
SS		
MS		
3,250	a game changer	
SS		
MS		
3,251	proved to be	
SS		
MS		
3,252	a slate of	
SS		
MS		

3,253	take a break	
SS		
MS		
3,254	a shift in strategy	
SS		
MS		
3,255	could lead to	
SS		
MS		
3,256	worried that	
SS		
MS		
3,257	briefed on	
SS		
MS		
3,258	could backfire	
SS		
MS		

3,259	express concern that	
SS		
MS		
3,260	retreat from	
SS		
MS		
3,261	take priority	
SS		
MS		
3,262	wait to see	
SS		
MS		
3,263	return a call	
SS		
MS		
3,264	failure to launch	
SS		
MS		

3,265	a budding writer	
SS		
MS		
3,266	not disclosed	
SS		
MS		
3,267	plan to move forward with	
SS		
MS		
3,268	absolutely spectacular	
SS		
MS		
3,269	part ways with	
SS		
MS		
3,270	joyful about	
SS		
MS		

3,271	cut against	
SS		
MS		
3,272	a valid reason	
SS		
MS		
3,273	a choppy relationship	
SS		
MS		
3,274	do an end-run around	
SS		
MS		
3,275	authoritarian government	
SS		
MS		
3,276	even when	
SS		
MS		

3,277	couldn't sleep	
SS		
MS		
3,278	expensive restaurants	
SS		
MS		
3,279	aim for	
SS		
MS		
3,280	exercise caution	
SS		
MS		
3,281	devoted to	
SS		
MS		
3,282	kept asking	
SS		
MS		

3,283	a large chunk of	
SS		
MS		
3,284	became hooked	
SS		
MS		
3,285	over the next few weeks	
SS		
MS		
3,286	prone to	
SS		
MS		
3,287	dabbled in	
SS		
MS		
3,288	efficient way of	
SS		
MS		

3,289	without the involvement of	
SS		
MS		
3,290	a type of	
SS		
MS		
3,291	highly successful	
SS		
MS		
3,292	reveal a lot about	
SS		
MS		
3,293	recall how	
SS		
MS		
3,294	cut relations with	
SS		
MS		

3,295	met with praise	
SS		
MS		
3,296	stepped up to	
SS		
MS		
3,297	watched with anticipation	
SS		
MS		
3,298	without realizing that	
SS		
MS		
3,299	silenced by	
SS		
MS		
3,300	a rift between	
SS		
MS		

3,301	preparing for	
SS		
MS		
3,302	could proceed	
SS		
MS		
3,303	have a threat hanging over	
SS		
MS		
3,304	move on from	
SS		
MS		
3,305	stood a chance of	
SS		
MS		
3,306	openly admitted	
SS		
MS		

3,307	difficult to prove	
SS		
MS		
3,308	gasped in surprise	
SS		
MS		
3,309	kept wondering	
SS		
MS		
3,310	keep wondering	
SS		
MS		
3,311	not waste too much time	
SS		
MS		
3,312	wiped out	
SS		
MS		

3,313	quite frivolous	
SS		
MS		
3,314	extravagant gifts	
SS		
MS		
3,315	off the record	
SS		
MS		
3,316	so critical	
SS		
MS		
3,317	toss the key	
SS		
MS		
3,318	looking back	
SS		
MS		

3,319	how deeply	
SS		
MS		
3,320	the average person	
SS		
MS		
3,321	inherently hazardous	
SS		
MS		
3,322	not honest	
SS		
MS		
3,323	a very long time	
SS		
MS		
3,324	tell lies	
SS		
MS		

3,325	standard operating procedure	
SS		
MS		
3,326	has a different take on	
SS		
MS		
3,327	nothing to hide	
SS		
MS		
3,328	likely course	
SS		
MS		
3,329	reduce reliance on	
SS		
MS		
3,330	not helping	
SS		
MS		

3,331	properly heard	
SS		
MS		
3,332	carbon emissions	
SS		
MS		
3,333	easy to see	
SS		
MS		
3,334	dramatically alter	
SS		
MS		
3,335	get behind	
SS		
MS		
3,336	hoping to	
SS		
MS		

3,337	standard bearer	
SS		
MS		
3,338	regularly support	
SS		
MS		
3,339	certainly think that	
SS		
MS		
3,340	huge savings	
SS		
MS		
3,341	purge of	
SS		
MS		
3,342	softball questions	
SS		
MS		

3,343	constant moaning	
SS		
MS		
3,344	reached an impasse	
SS		
MS		
3,345	become a lightning rod for	
SS		
MS		
3,346	a powerful moment	
SS		
MS		
3,347	felt different	
SS		
MS		
3,348	flinch from	
SS		
MS		

3,349	in unusual circumstances	
SS		
MS		
3,350	pose a danger	
SS		
MS		
3,351	seems beyond question	
SS		
MS		
3,352	a risky tour	
SS		
MS		
3,353	became a fixture at	
SS		
MS		
3,354	rose to prominence	
SS		
MS		

3,355	needed time for	
SS		
MS		
3,356	try to put together	
SS		
MS		
3,357	curious to know	
SS		
MS		
3,358	had the chops for	
SS		
MS		
3,359	regular appearance	
SS		
MS		
3,360	talking heads	
SS		
MS		

3,361	all at once	
SS		
MS		
3,362	barely notice	
SS		
MS		
3,363	ordinary people	
SS		
MS		
3,364	populated with	
SS		
MS		
3,365	hard to know	
SS		
MS		
3,366	tasked with	
SS		
MS		

3,367	barely contemplate	
SS		
MS		
3,368	unprepared to handle	
SS		
MS		
3,369	a jarring reminder	
SS		
MS		
3,370	call a halt to	
SS		
MS		
3,371	not medically necessary	
SS		
MS		
3,372	horrified by	
SS		
MS		

3,373	incensed by	
SS		
MS		
3,374	divulge information	
SS		
MS		
3,375	successfully altered	
SS		
MS		
3,376	never let on that	
SS		
MS		
3,377	had some concerns about	
SS		
MS		
3,378	incredibly challenging	
SS		
MS		

3,379	a natural affinity for	
SS		
MS		
3,380	take an inventory of	
SS		
MS		
3,381	initiated by	
SS		
MS		
3,382	a catastrophic event	
SS		
MS		
3,383	a constant influx of	
SS		
MS		
3,384	military base	
SS		
MS		

3,385	began questioning	
SS		
MS		
3,386	exceedingly simple	
SS		
MS		
3,387	the entire area	
SS		
MS		
3,388	as night came on	
SS		
MS		
3,389	indebted to	
SS		
MS		
3,390	the parting crowd	
SS		
MS		

3,391	march in procession	
SS		
MS		
3,392	it was in vain that	
SS		
MS		
3,393	gave me little joy	
SS		
MS		
3,394	grew so rapidly	
SS		
MS		
3,395	tardiness in	
SS		
MS		
3,396	purporting to	
SS		
MS		

3,397	public opinion	
SS		
MS		
3,398	never again	
SS		
MS		
3,399	bid adieu	
SS		
MS		
3,400	seat yourself	
SS		
MS		
3,401	fulfil the promise	
SS		
MS		
3,402	daily labour	
SS		
MS		

3,403	a deep sleep	
SS		
MS		
3,404	remedial action	
SS		
MS		
3,405	pleaded guilty	
SS		
MS		
3,406	last several weeks	
SS		
MS		
3,407	steal the limelight	
SS		
MS		
3,408	do themselves no favours by	
SS		
MS		

3,409	an ongoing conflict	
SS		
MS		
3,410	on the grounds of	
SS		
MS		
3,411	on a large scale	
SS		
MS		
3,412	gloss over	
SS		
MS		
3,413	set a limit	
SS		
MS		
3,414	not incapable	
SS		
MS		

3,415	a horrible message	
SS		
MS		
3,416	learn valuable lessons	
SS		
MS		
3,417	a leave of absence	
SS		
MS		
3,418	head up	
SS		
MS		
3,419	little understood by	
SS		
MS		
3,420	is ostensibly about	
SS		
MS		

3,421	synonymous with	
SS		
MS		
3,422	in the course of	
SS		
MS		
3,423	the more important question is	
SS		
MS		
3,424	quite a sight	
SS		
MS		
3,425	make a point of	
SS		
MS		
3,426	in order to	
SS		
MS		

3,427	rarely interrupt	
SS		
MS		
3,428	cultural practice	
SS		
MS		
3,429	has no experience with	
SS		
MS		
3,430	provides an overview of	
SS		
MS		
3,431	in furtherance of	
SS		
MS		
3,432	there is a growing appreciation for	
SS		
MS		

3,433	what I find remarkable about X is	
SS		
MS		
3,434	without restriction	
SS		
MS		
3,435	boost security	
SS		
MS		
3,436	qualified support	
SS		
MS		
3,437	at all costs	
SS		
MS		
3,438	interwoven with	
SS		
MS		

3,439	a nod to	
SS		
MS		
3,440	it gave me great pleasure to	
SS		
MS		
3,441	has great merit	
SS		
MS		
3,442	renew attempt to	
SS		
MS		
3,443	forbidden fruit	
SS		
MS		
3,444	a horrible scene	
SS		
MS		

3,445	increase substantially	
SS		
MS		
3,446	having a really difficult time	
SS		
MS		
3,447	upsetting to	
SS		
MS		
3,448	fascination with	
SS		
MS		
3,449	notified of	
SS		
MS		
3,450	equitable workplace	
SS		
MS		

3,451	eager to begin	
SS		
MS		
3,452	retracted a job offer	
SS		
MS		
3,453	not caught immediately	
SS		
MS		
3,454	completely unacceptable	
SS		
MS		
3,455	dole out	
SS		
MS		
3,456	happen upon	
SS		
MS		

3,457	not infrequently	
SS		
MS		
3,458	over the top	
SS		
MS		
3,459	riveting story	
SS		
MS		
3,460	one of those people	
SS		
MS		
3,461	an extraordinary woman	
SS		
MS		
3,462	personal fulfilment	
SS		
MS		

3,463	no one seemed more surprised than	
SS		
MS		
3,464	take a little time	
SS		
MS		
3,465	the sweet spot	
SS		
MS		
3,466	hugely popular with	
SS		
MS		
3,467	doesn't pass the smell test	
SS		
MS		
3,468	claim to fame	
SS		
MS		

3,469	far more interesting than	
SS		
MS		
3,470	a no-go zone	
SS		
MS		
3,471	tend to disappear	
SS		
MS		
3,472	sheer ignorance	
SS		
MS		
3,473	very much in contrast with	
SS		
MS		
3,474	is a feature, not a bug	
SS		
MS		

3,475	scrambled to	
SS		
MS		
3,476	hinge on	
SS		
MS		
3,477	screw up	
SS		
MS		
3,478	made an oral argument	
SS		
MS		
3,479	walk back	
SS		
MS		
3,480	make a strong case for	
SS		
MS		

3,481	hemming and hawing	
SS		
MS		
3,482	an honest answer	
SS		
MS		
3,483	may not wear so well	
SS		
MS		
3,484	makes an excellent point	
SS		
MS		
3,485	out of step	
SS		
MS		
3,486	might not last	
SS		
MS		

3,487	make a decision	
SS		
MS		
3,488	crowded field	
SS		
MS		
3,489	beloved by	
SS		
MS		
3,490	absolutely correct	
SS		
MS		
3,491	forfeiture of	
SS		
MS		
3,492	stumbled upon	
SS		
MS		

3,493	held in custody	
SS		
MS		
3,494	took too long	
SS		
MS		
3,495	forced to admit	
SS		
MS		
3,496	for a few weeks now	
SS		
MS		
3,497	no skin in the game	
SS		
MS		
3,498	started off	
SS		
MS		

3,499	reeled off	
SS		
MS		
3,500	an amazing insight	
SS		
MS		
3,501	a tough fight	
SS		
MS		
3,502	incapable of	
SS		
MS		
3,503	security risk	
SS		
MS		
3,504	there is no better test of X than	
SS		
MS		

3,505	there is no sign that	
SS		
MS		
3,506	there is no sign of	
SS		
MS		
3,507	rental assistance payments	
SS		
MS		
3,508	unpaid leave	
SS		
MS		
3,509	a meaningful life	
SS		
MS		
3,510	moral excellence	
SS		
MS		

3,511	put tremendous effort into	
SS		
MS		
3,512	the most difficult job	
SS		
MS		
3,513	an outpouring of grief	
SS		
MS		
3,514	common knowledge	
SS		
MS		
3,515	exist in great abundance	
SS		
MS		
3,516	multiple factors	
SS		
MS		

3,517	an impressive accomplishment	
SS		
MS		
3,518	was touted as	
SS		
MS		
3,519	the first ever	
SS		
MS		
3,520	undying gratitude	
SS		
MS		
3,521	scathing rebuke	
SS		
MS		
3,522	snide remark	
SS		
MS		

3,523	champion of	
SS		
MS		
3,524	not mincing word	
SS		
MS		
3,525	most glaring	
SS		
MS		
3,526	blistering comment	
SS		
MS		
3,527	get an earful from	
SS		
MS		
3,528	adamant about	
SS		
MS		

3,529	indigenous to	
SS		
MS		
3,530	secured at	
SS		
MS		
3,531	refreshing to	
SS		
MS		
3,532	quest for	
SS		
MS		
3,533	know nothing about	
SS		
MS		
3,534	it takes time to	
SS		
MS		

3,535	pessimistic about	
SS		
MS		
3,536	an enlightening experience	
SS		
MS		
3,537	the ideal place	
SS		
MS		
3,538	throw one's hat in the ring	
SS		
MS		
3,539	a contender for	
SS		
MS		
3,540	stretch the truth	
SS		
MS		

3,541	visible from	
SS		
MS		
3,542	strongly defended	
SS		
MS		
3,543	speak out against	
SS		
MS		
3,544	it is unclear whether	
SS		
MS		
3,545	stake out a position on	
SS		
MS		
3,546	immediately respond	
SS		
MS		

3,547	a thoughtless claim	
SS		
MS		
3,548	the abandonment of	
SS		
MS		
3,549	cause dismay	
SS		
MS		
3,550	sharply criticized	
SS		
MS		
3,551	done incalculable damage to	
SS		
MS		
3,552	dismissive attitude to	
SS		
MS		

3,553	has had its day	
SS		
MS		
3,554	akin to	
SS		
MS		
3,555	most of the world	
SS		
MS		
3,556	hardly equivalent to	
SS		
MS		
3,557	a quarter of	
SS		
MS		
3,558	has sharply declined	
SS		
MS		

3,559	get tangled in	
SS		
MS		
3,560	at a worrisome level	
SS		
MS		
3,561	hamper efforts to	
SS		
MS		
3,562	withdrawal from	
SS		
MS		
3,563	an outlier	
SS		
MS		
3,564	there is no justification for	
SS		
MS		

3,565	started crying	
SS		
MS		
3,566	it's hard to pinpoint	
SS		
MS		
3,567	ethnically ambiguous	
SS		
MS		
3,568	the early stage of	
SS		
MS		
3,569	end badly	
SS		
MS		
3,570	evicted from	
SS		
MS		

About the Author

Everett Ofori holds an MBA from Heriot-Watt University (Scotland, UK) and a Master of Science, Finance, from the College for Financial Planning, Colorado, USA. He teaches Public Speaking, Management, Marketing, and English for Specific Purposes (Business Writing, Medical Writing, Meeting Facilitation, etc.). Everett has helped hundreds of high school and university students around the world to improve their writing and grades. He has also worked extensively with business executives (including those at the C-level).

Everett has worked with clients/students from the following organizations and more:

Accenture	Actelion	Asahi Kasei Medical
Asahi Soft Drink Research, Moriya	Astellas	Bandai
Barclays	Becton Dickinson	Chugai/Roche Pharmaceutical
Disney	ExxonMobil	Fujitsu
Gyao	Goldman Sachs	Hitachi Automotive
Hitachi Design	IIJ (Internet Initiative Japan)	Johnson & Johnson (Janssen)
JP Morgan	JVCKenwood	L'Oreal
McKinsey Japan Mitsubishi (Shoji)	Moody's	National Institute of Land and Infrastructure Management, Tsukuba, Japan (NILIM)
Nomura	Orix	PriceWaterhouseCoopers (PWC)
Recruit	Reinsurance Group of America (RGA)	Sekizenkai Nursing School, Shimosoga, Kanagawa
Sumisho	Summit Agro International	Sumitomo
Suntory	Tokyo International Business College, Asakusabashi, Tokyo W. L. Gore	Yahoo Japan
Yokohama Child Welfare College (Hoiku Fukushi), Higashi-Totsuka, Kanagawa		

www.ingramcontent.com/pod-product-compliance
Lightning Source LLC
Chambersburg PA
CBHW080020110526
44587CB00021BA/3417